KT-168-992

POCKET
GARDENING
GUIDES

HERBACEOUS
PERENNIALS

— ❖ —

DAVID SQUIRE

POCKET
GARDENING
GUIDES

HERBACEOUS PERENNIALS

❖

DAVID SQUIRE

Illustrated by Vana Haggerty

TIGER BOOKS INTERNATIONAL
LONDON

Designed and conceived by

THE BRIDGEWATER BOOK COMPANY LTD

Art Directed by PETER BRIDGEWATER

Designed by TERRY JEAVONS

Illustrated by VANA HAGGERTY FLS

Edited by MARGOT RICHARDSON

Managing Editor ANNA CLARKSON

CLB 3507

This edition published in 1995 by

TIGER BOOKS INTERNATIONAL PLC, London

© 1995 Colour Library Books Ltd,

Godalming, Surrey

Printed and bound in Singapore

All rights reserved

ISBN 1-85501-419-X

CONTENTS

DEVELOPMENT OF
HERBACEOUS BORDERS

❖

WITH THE introduction and passion for exotic half-hardy annuals during the 1820s and early 1830s, it was predicted by the middle of the century that herbaceous perennials would cease to be grown. Perennials had formed a major part of 'old-fashioned' gardens and perhaps owed their early survival to monastic establishments. This prognosis, perhaps given by those gardeners dedicated only to bedding plants, was totally inaccurate. Although in most large gardens bedding plants, sometimes displayed in intricate patterns, were grown enthusiastically, traditional herbaceous borders were also continued. Also, perennials were still grown in nurseries, so maintaining a reservoir of good plants.

DEATH MYTH

The Irish gardener and writer William Robinson (1838–1935), although an advocate of herbaceous borders, appears to have encouraged the myth that by the 1880s herbaceous plants had all but disappeared from gardens. He later inferred that their rediscovery was solely due to cottage gardens which, by their nature, had always been a repository of plants with different natures. And by the end of the first decade of the 1900s he was claiming to have been almost totally responsible for the resurgence of interest in them!

Nevertheless, his writings, which were fortunate enough to coincide with a general hunger for gardening information and a popularization of the printed word, did generate interest in herbaceous plants. And his book *The English Flower Garden*, published in 1883, went to fifteen editions during his lifetime, and several more later. Also, he wrote widely in garden

———

ENGRAVINGS *of herbaceous borders in the 1870s reveal general informality and clearly indicate that earlier claims of the imminent demise of these plants was untrue. Engravings similar to this modern representation were featured by herbaceous-plant nurserymen in their catalogues.*

GERTRUDE JEKYLL

Perhaps the name most associated with herbaceous plants and borders is the English garden designer Gertrude Jekyll (1843–1932). She came to gardening fairly late in life; earlier she had thoughts of being a painter but progressive myopia prevented her painting on canvas, so she took up designing with plants.

Her partnership with the young architect Edwin Lutyens increased her designing experience and a Lutyens house and Jekyll garden became very desirable.

Much of her designing philosophy was based on traditional cottage gardens, which she acknowledged when writing: 'they have a simple and tender charm that one may look for in vain in gardens of greater pretension. And the old garden flowers seem to know that there they are seen at their best.'

Red Hot Pokers and cannas were two of the plants frequently featured in Gertrude Jekyll's borders. Between them they introduced bright flower colours and vibrantly colourful leaves.

magazines. His influence was – and has been – important, introducing informality to gardens and advocating 'mixed' planting. He also examined a softer and more subtle use of colour. Arranging plants in attractive combinations was another of his passions.

OTHER AUTHORS

It must be stressed that *The English Flower Garden* included chapters by three other writers, whose thoughts about colour did not always coincide with Robinson's. Two of these advocates were William Wildsmith and J.D. (thought to be J. Dundas). Gertrude Jekyll was the other writer, who lived about the same time as Robinson but came later to gardening. She introduced more of a painter's influence to herbaceous borders, and popularized the planting of large, informal drifts of colour and colour schemes based on complementary colours. Single-colour borders were another of her passions and introductions.

Miss Jekyll was keen to make the virtues of herbaceous plants widely known and her first book was published in 1899. Others followed, detailing the use of colour schemes and even the planting of borders with just one colour theme. Many gardens still have a rich legacy of planting schemes which originated from her ideas.

Her enthusiasm and use of herbaceous perennials was said to have eclipsed the general use of half-hardy bedding plants that had been widely featured in gardens in the middle of the nineteenth century. However, in her last years, Miss Jekyll often paid tribute to bedding plants.

WHAT ARE
HERBACEOUS PERENNIALS?

❖

HERBACEOUS perennials are plants that each spring develop fresh shoots which grow and bear flowers before the onset of cold weather in late autumn. Their leaves and stems then die down, leaving the root part dormant during winter. However, most herbaceous borders are not so 'pure of spirit' and invariably become homes for other types of plants, perhaps bulbous-based or with a slightly woody nature. Even small bamboos are frequently included. This *pot-pourri* approach to herbaceous borders may not create one with a thoroughbred nature, but does produce a varied range of flowers, leaves and seed-pods. And it is this mixed nature that often enables borders to remain attractive over a long period and to create such a spectacular display right through to the frosts of autumn – or later.

HERBAL NATURE

Many of the plants now grown in herbaceous borders were once considered to have medicinal or domestic uses. Balm (Melissa officinalis) *was used as a strewing herb to repel fleas and lice and to create a pleasing aroma, as well as being employed for its culinary qualities. The Oxe-eye Chamomile (*Anthemis tinctoria)*, also known as Dyer's Chamomile, was used to produce a yellow dye, while the blue flowers of Borage* (Borago officinalis) *were added to ales to produce a 'cooling' taste. Tansy* (Tanacetum vulgare)*, now often grown in the form 'Crispum', was earlier used to make pudding and cakes.*

ACANTHUS MOLLIS *(Bear's Breeches) is an herbaceous plant well known for its dominant spires of flowers and large, deeply cut leaves that are said to have inspired early architecture.*

AGAPANTHUS, *mainly from South Africa, has fleshy roots and a slightly tender nature. Plants are soon damaged by frost and normally need a sheltered position. However, the 'Headbourne Hybrids' are slightly hardier.*

CENTRANTHUS RUBER *is a European native earlier known as* Kentranthus ruber. *It was introduced into Britain and soon become naturalized. Commonly, it is known as Red Valerian and valued for its red or deep pink flowers.*

CLEMATIS HERACLEIFOLIA *is an herbaceous species of clematis originally from China. It displays clusters of tubular, purple-blue flowers during mid and late summer on plants up to 90cm/3ft high. Sometimes it is grown on supports formed of twiggy pea sticks.*

KNIPHOFIAS *are widely known as Torch Lilies and Red Hot Pokers. Like many herbaceous plants, the garden hybrids now far exceed the species in general cultivation. However, all Torch Lilies have similar flowers, resembling pokers.*

SMILACINA RACEMOSA *is, like many herbaceous perennials, native to North America. Known as the False Spikenard, it develops terminal sprays of scented, creamy-white flowers on arching stems. It is an ideal plant for planting in moist soil and light shade.*

TROLLIUS *x* HYBRIDUS, *one of the Globe Flowers, is a cross between two species and the parent of many superb varieties which have globe-shaped flowers and a wide colour range. The British and European native T. europeaus was the first Globe Flower known in European Gardens.*

ZANTEDESCHIA AETHIOPICA, *the Arum Lily, is a relatively tender plant that in temperate and exposed climates needs protection during winter. Like many other plants with hardier forms, this too has one in the variety 'Crowborough'. This has encouraged its much wider use in flower beds.*

PLANTS THAT TEST THE RULE

Proper herbaceous plants die down to soil level in late autumn or early winter, but what of Lamb's Tongue and bergenias, both well-known residents of herbaceous borders? The Lamb's Tongue *(Stachys byzantina)* has large, tongue-shaped leaves densely covered with white, silvery hairs throughout winter. Bergenias, descriptively known as Elephant's Ears, have persistent, leathery leaves that look superb when covered in frost.

It must be remembered that the term herbaceous may, in some cases, be just a gardener's classification for a plant that when grown in a temperate climate is not sufficiently hardy to survive with all its leaves still in place. For

example, Mediterranean plants often assume an herbaceous nature in cold climates, whereas in their native land they maintain leaves throughout the year.

Dahlias are popular in herbaceous borders, but the tubers are not able to withstand winters in temperate climates, even when insulated by several inches of soil. The tubers are therefore lifted immediately frost blackens the foliage, and placed in a frost-proof, dry shed. In spring or early summer they are divided and replanted into flower borders.

It is clear that to encompass the widest possible range of so-called herbaceous plants, gardeners need a pragmatic rather than a purist attitude. It is with this view in mind that the plants in this book have been selected.

USING
HERBACEOUS PERENNIALS

❖

H ERBACEOUS perennials are very adaptable and although usually used in borders backed by a hedge they can also be planted in other parts of gardens.

TRADITIONAL BORDERS

These are borders 1.8m/6ft or more wide and usually backed by an evergreen hedge such as Yew. A variation on this is double-sided borders formed of two flower beds on either side of a broad grass path. An alternative to grass is a wide paved area formed of well-weathered flag stones. The hedges protect plants from cold winds, as well as creating a pleasing background throughout the year. Unfortunately, borders such as these, totally dedicated to herbaceous perennials, are now a rarity.

MIXED BORDERS

These are formed mainly of herbaceous perennials, but also annuals, biennials and shrubs. Hedges can be used as a background, but cordon as well as

PROTECTING
LAWN EDGES

Many herbaceous plants have a low, cascading nature that makes them ideal for the edges of borders. Unfortunately, when plants are positioned close to a lawn's edge the grass is invariably killed, leaving bare patches that are especially evident during winter. This can be avoided by placing a row of paving slabs along the edge. Plants can then be positioned right up to the border's edge. Also, the slabs make it easier to dig or fork over a border without tipping soil on the grass.

bush fruit trees are a possibility and introduce a relaxed and informal cottage-garden atmosphere. However, when using fruit trees, ensure that plants are not deprived of light and circulating air around them.

TRADITIONALLY, *herbaceous borders were planted solely with herbaceous perennials. This meant that during winter the entire border was bare; the plants persisted through their dormant roots.*

MIXED BORDERS *are increasingly popular and are formed of a range of herbaceous perennials, annuals and biennials, bulbs, shrubs and even small trees. This system creates colour throughout the year.*

HERBACEOUS PLANTS *are ideal for planting alongside streams and ponds. Many plants survive or even thrive in these persistently moist positions, and some of them are suggested on pages 40 and 41.*

LOW-GROWING PLANTS *smother the ground, creating a carpet of attractive leaves and, in some cases, flowers. Some of these plants have leaves that persist throughout winter, others just during the summer months.*

WOODLAND GARDENS, *where plants grow under a light canopy of tall, deciduous trees, provide homes for many shade-loving herbaceous plants. Some of these plants are described on pages 38 and 39.*

SINGLE-SIDED BORDERS, *where plants are grown in a border and with a wall, fence or hedge along the back, are a traditional way to grow herbaceous plants. Double-sided borders are popular.*

WATERSIDE PLANTS

The edges of ponds are frequently paved to form firm standing areas from where fish and aquatic plants can be admired. However, it is also possible to plant moist areas around natural or man-made ponds with moisture-loving herbaceous plants as well as some border primulas. Bog gardens help to integrate a pond with its surroundings and together they form a dominant feature with a wide range of plants. Some have attractive flowers, while others display colourful or large leaves.

WOODLAND AND GROUND COVER

Many herbaceous plants happily grow in shade. They can be successfully grown with bulbous plants between shrubs and under a light, leafy canopy, preferably created by deciduous trees. This allows soil to receive rain during winter and sunshine in spring and early summer. A total canopy of evergreen trees keeps the soil too dry and the area excessively dark. Many ground-covering plants thrive in these conditions; a range is suggested on pages 32 and 33.

BORDER SHAPE

ISLAND BEDS, *usually kidney shaped and set within a lawn, are mainly planted with herbaceous plants that do not need to be supported by twiggy sticks. A range of them is detailed on pages 30 and 31.*

SINGLE ISLAND BEDS *can be integrated, even into small lawns. They are usually positioned towards a corner so that a focal point is created and the lawn is not fragmented into several small pieces.*

ISLAND BEDS *should be between 1.8m/6ft and 2.4m/8ft at their widest points. This enables the soil to be hoed without having to walk all over it.*

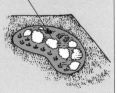

PREPARING THE SITE

❖

THERE is no substitute for thoroughly digging and preparing a flower bed in early winter. It ensures good drainage, enables compost or manure to be mixed with the soil, and provides an opportunity to remove the roots of perennial weeds, such as thistles, docks and horsetails.

Single digging, when the soil is cultivated to the depth of a single spade's blade (about 25cm/10in), is usually sufficient. Double digging is only necessary when converting pasture land to a garden. But it is especially desirable when there is an impervious layer of soil a couple of feet below the surface. Double digging involves cultivating soil to the depth of two spade blades, but not mixing the layers.

Dig soil in early winter: it is not necessary to break up the surface, as exposure to frost, wind and rain will break it down by spring, one of the times to put in new plants (see pages 22 and 23).

Do not walk on the soil's surface during winter, as this consolidates it unevenly, excluding air, preventing rapid drainage and early warming in spring.

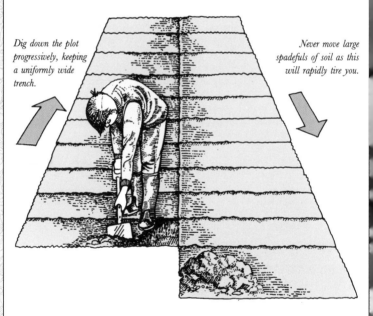

Dig down the plot progressively, keeping a uniformly wide trench.

Never move large spadefuls of soil as this will rapidly tire you.

WHEN *digging a wide border, use a garden line to divide it lengthways into two equally sized pieces. Then, dig a trench 30cm/12in wide and to the depth of a spade's blade across one half of the plot. Put soil from this trench on the other side of the plot (as shown).*

THIS *dug out soil will be used to fill the last trench on the other side when digging is complete. Start digging across the trench, systematically inverting spadefuls of soil (see top of page 13 for details), so that the position of the trench moves progressively down the plot.*

WHEN *the end of the first of the two strips is reached, use soil from the trench on the opposite side to fill it. Then, dig down the second side of the plot. Finally, fill the last of the trenches with the soil that was removed from the first trench on the other side of the plot.*

1. WHEN *single digging, first take out a trench to the depth of a spade's blade and about 30cm/12in wide. It is essential when digging a border that a trench is maintained, as manure and compost can then be put into it and buried.*

2. INSERT *the spade's blade vertically into the soil, so that each time a block 7.5–10cm/3–4in is removed and turned over. On light soil, larger pieces can be dug, while for clay soil slightly smaller slices of soil are much more manageable.*

3. DIGGING *is a repetitive operation and if too large pieces are dug, or for an excessively long time, back strain can occur. Keeping the spade's blade clean makes the work more pleasurable. And always entirely remove all perennial weeds.*

SOIL PESTS

While digging, take the opportunity to pick up and destroy soil pests such as cockchafer grubs (usually curled, fleshy and plump, dirty creamy-white), wireworms (slim, yellow-brown, shiny and horny skinned) and leatherjackets (brownish-grey, legless and tough-skinned). They can also be exposed on the soil's surface and left for birds to eat. Digging invariably attracts birds and they patiently wait as digging progresses, darting here and there and picking up and eating grubs.

During the 1950s and 60s chemical pesticides were proclaimed to be the panacea for the eradication of garden pests and to be the epitome of good gardening, but it is cheaper and much more environmentally friendly to rely on nature to kill them than to spray and dust plants continually throughout the summer.

DIGGING WITHOUT STRAIN

Automatic spades are available and an excellent investment, especially if you have a weak back. The spade has a T-shaped handle and a lever action that virtually eliminates lifting and bending. After inserting the blade in the ground, a pull on the handlebars throws soil forward into the trench, at the same time inverting it. An alternative is to hire or buy a motor-driven cultivator, but using them on hard or stony ground is exceptionally difficult work.

RAISING NEW PLANTS

❖

MANY herbaceous perennials can be raised from seeds: some are sown in gentle warmth in greenhouses during spring, others under the protection of garden frames in late spring, and others in seed-beds in the open, without the benefit of added warmth.

Clearly, the method most available to home gardeners is to form a seed-bed in well-drained but moisture-retentive soil in a bright, sheltered corner. After seeds are sown, keep the seed-bed moist but not waterlogged. If birds are a problem, stretch white cotton across the bed or temporarily place twiggy sticks on the soil. When the seedlings are established, thin them in two stages to between 15cm/6in and 30cm/12in apart (see opposite page).

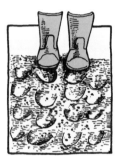

1. IN SPRING, *rake a piece of soil level (previously dug – see pages 12 and 13) to form a seed-bed. Then, systematically tread over it to ensure even compaction. Do not use a garden roller for this job.*

2. RAKE *the surface level, at the same time removing large stones. Do not remove them all, as they are essential to the well-being of soil. It may be necessary to rake the soil in several directions to make it level.*

3. STRETCH *a garden line across the plot and use a stick or draw hoe to form drills 6–12cm/ 1/4–1/2in deep. Space these drills 15–23cm/ 6–9in apart, and ensure that the ends of the rows are clearly marked.*

4. THINLY *and evenly sow seeds in a straight line in the drill's base. Ensure they do not fall in clusters, as this is a waste and makes thinning the subsequent seedlings even more essential.*

5. COVER *the seeds: either straddle the row and use your feet to guide soil over the seeds, or employ the back of a rake. Then, shallowly rake along the direction of the drill, not across the row.*

6. FIRM *soil over the row: either shuffle sideways along the row, or use the top of a metal garden rake to settle soil around and over the seeds. Check that the ends of the rows are labelled.*

SEED-BED CARE

Throughout summer it is essential to remove weeds from between the plants and rows. If left, they steal moisture and food, congest seedlings and harbour pests and diseases. When removing weeds, place them in a box and later put on a compost heap. Also, when pulled out, their roots may loosen soil around herbaceous seedlings. Re-firm it around them and lightly water the rows.

Check plants regularly for pests eating leaves and chewing stems, often causing seedlings to collapse. Many pests and diseases are detailed on pages 58 and 59.

As soon as seedlings are large enough, thin them out (see below). By late autumn, they will have developed into plants that can be put into their flowering positions. It is also possible to leave planting until spring, when the weather is more conducive to rapid establishment of plants (see pages 22 and 23 for planting information).

THINNING SEEDLINGS

After seeds germinate, the seedlings are thinned to give those that remain more light and air. If left, they become congested, thin and weak and likely to be diseased. The distances apart depend on the size of the plants, but as an indication, those of Columbine (Aquilegia vulgaris) are first thinned to 7.5cm/3in apart, then 15cm/6in; while those of Anchusa azurea and Achillea filipendulina to twice these distances. Clearly, the larger the plants, the further the distance apart they are thinned.

PLANTS TO RAISE FROM SEEDS

There are many herbaceous plants that can be raised from seeds sown in seed-beds:
• Achillea filipendulina/A. millefolium/A. ptarmica: *6mm/¼in deep; late spring to early summer.*
• Agrimonia eupatoria: *6mm/¼in deep; late spring.*
• Anchusa azurea: *12mm/½in deep; late spring to early summer.*
• Aquilegia vulgaris: *6mm/¼in deep; late spring to early summer.*
• Aster novi-belgii: *12mm/½in deep; late spring.*
• Catananche caerulea: *6mm/¼in deep; late spring to early summer.*
• Centranthus ruber: *6mm/¼in deep; late spring to early summer.*
• Chrysanthemum maximum: *6mm/¼in deep; late spring to mid-summer.*
• Coreopsis grandiflora: *6mm/¼in deep; early summer.*
• Echinops ritro: *12mm/½in deep; late spring to early summer.*
• Erigeron speciosum: *6mm/¼in deep; late spring to mid-summer.*
• Incarvillea delavayi: *6mm/¼in deep; mid to late spring.*
• Linum narbonense: *6mm/¼in deep; early to mid-summer.*
• Lychnis chalcedonica/L. coronaria: *6mm/¼in deep; late spring to early summer.*
• Nepeta x faassenii: *6mm/¼in deep; early summer.*
• Papaver alpinum/P. nudicaule/P. orientale: *6mm/¼in deep; early summer.*

DIVIDING ESTABLISHED PLANTS

❖

IVISION is an easy and quick way to create further plants. It is also essential to divide established clumps every three or four years to ensure that relatively young plants are always present in a border. Otherwise they slowly deteriorate, their centres become woody and the quality of flowers clearly diminishes.

SPRING OR AUTUMN

Some fibrous-rooted herbaceous plants are divided in spring, others in autumn. Those divided in autumn are plants that flower early in the year which include doronicums, mertensias, pulmonarias and trollius. By dividing and replanting them in autumn, they are given the longest possible time in which to establish themselves before they flower.

Many plants can be divided in either autumn or spring, including geraniums, geums, heleniums,

> ## ALL HEAL
>
> Valerian officinalis, *also known as St. George's Herb and Phu, has long been grown in borders and was especially recommended in the Victorian era. During mediaeval times the roots were widely used medicinally and the plant became known as All Heal. The name Phu is said to derive from the first century physician Dioscorides (born in Asia Minor), who recommended its roots but was not impressed by the offensive aroma given off by them.*

lysimachias, macleayas, potentillas and solidagos. Other plants, such as pyrethrums, scabious, Shasta Daisy *(Chrysanthemum maximum)* and late-flowering asters are best divided in spring.

1. LARGE *clumps of fibrous-rooted herbaceous perennials can be lifted and divided in autumn or spring (see above for the types best suited to specific times). Place the clump on a piece of canvas and insert two garden forks, back-to-back.*

2. LEVER *the handles of the forks together, so that the fibrous roots are pulled apart. When these are loose, only then pull the handles apart. If the handles are first levered outwards, this tears the shoots apart but does not loosen the roots.*

3. USE *your hands to pull plants apart, retaining young pieces from around the outside and discarding old parts at the plant's centre. Do not pull plants into very small pieces; a few good sized plants are better than numerous weedy ones.*

1. SMALL, *fibrous-rooted clumps of plants such as Michaelmas Daisies can usually be pulled apart by hand. Cutting plants down earlier to just above soil level aids their division.*

2. PULL *the crowns into pieces that form good sized plants. Pull away old roots that have become matted and twisted. Also, check them to ensure they are not contaminated with pests.*

3. DISCARD *old pieces that were formerly at the plant's centre. The best flowers are always produced on young parts and it is therefore essential only to replant these pieces into borders.*

Some plants, such as bearded irises, which include the London Flag *(Iris germanica)*, polyanthus and epimediums, are best divided immediately after they finish flowering, although the London Flag can also be propagated in late summer.

Plants such as bearded irises, Day Lilies *(hemerocallis)*, agapanthus and paeonies form dense clumps and after being carefully lifted from the soil a sharp knife is essential to separate the thick, tough roots.

RAPID ESTABLISHMENT

Whether division is in spring or autumn, never divide plants if the soil is frozen, excessively wet or very dry; if dry, it is necessary to water plants regularly until they are established. More young plants fail to become established because their roots become dry than for any other reason.

If plants are divided into very small pieces, it is better to put them into a nurserybed for a year or two before setting them in borders. Later, when put into a border, they will create a much more impressive display. When put into a nurserybed, always ensure the plants are labelled.

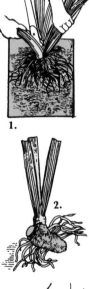

BEARDED IRISES, *like the London Flag* (Iris germanica), *are popular border plants. Divide them immediately after they finish flowering in early summer, or wait until late summer.*
1. *Carefully use a garden fork to dig up the entire clump (top, left). Take care not to pierce or bruise the roots.*
2. *Use a sharp knife to cut the rhizomes (thick, concertina-like roots), so that each part has one, two or three fans of leaves (centre, left). Cut these 15–20cm/ 6–8in long, also severing long roots.*
3. *Replant them 30–38cm/12–15in apart, with the top of the rhizome only just covered. Use your feet to firm the soil around them (bottom, left).*

CUTTINGS & LAYERING

❖

MANY plants grown in herbaceous borders can be increased from cuttings taken either from shoots or roots. Chrysanthemum and dahlia cuttings are detailed on pages 20 and 21, while those of delphiniums are on the opposite page. Taking root-cuttings is less well known but is equally efficient.

ROOT-CUTTINGS

There are several plants with thick roots that can be encouraged to form new roots. These include anchusas, *Anemone hupehensis*, Cupid's Dart *(Catananche caerulea)*, eryngiums, lupins, Oriental Poppy *(Papaver orientale)*, romneyas and verbascums.

Root-cuttings enable a large number of new plants to be produced from a single parent. Normally, taking root-cuttings means that the mother plant is virtually destroyed while yielding cuttings, but it is possible to dig

> ### HORMONE
> ### ROOTING POWDERS
>
> *These enable cut surfaces to form roots rapidly, and are especially beneficial for soft-wood cuttings and layers. Tip a small amount of powder into a lid and dip in the bases of cuttings. With layers, dust the cut surfaces.*

down on one side of a plant and to remove carefully a few healthy roots. Nevertheless, this is an exception, rather than the norm.

The roots when cut into 7.5–10cm/3–4in-long pieces must be inserted in compost so that the end nearest the crown is uppermost. This is assured by slicing the end nearest to a root's tip with a sloping cut, and using a flat cut on the other end. Should several cuttings become mixed, it is then easy to sort them out.

THICK ROOT-CUTTINGS

1. PLANTS *with thick roots can be increased by digging them up during their dormant period in autumn or winter. Suitable plants are indicated above. First, clean and wash the roots. Only use healthy, undamaged pieces.*

2. CUT *the roots into pieces 5–7.5cm/2–3in long, making a flat cut at the end nearest the plant's crown, and a slant at the other. Insert these, flat side uppermost, in a mixture of equal parts moist peat and sharp sand.*

3. PRESS *each cutting into the compost so that its top is level with the surface. Then, lightly sieve 6–12mm/¼–½in of compost over them, water and place in a cold frame. When shoots appear, pot up the cuttings.*

1. TAKE *delphinium cuttings in spring. Use a sharp knife to sever 7.5–10cm/3–4in-long shoots, cutting them close to the plant's base.*

2. TRIM *off the lower leaves and insert the cuttings 2.5–3.6cm/1–1½in deep in equal parts moist peat and sharp sand. Use a 12mm/½in-thick dibber.*

3. PUT *four or five cuttings in a 13cm/5in-wide pot, positioning them 12mm/½in from the side. Firm the compost, then water and place in a cold frame.*

THIN ROOT-CUTTINGS

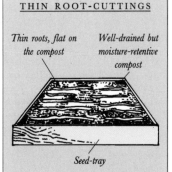

Thin roots, flat on the compost

Well-drained but moisture-retentive compost

Seed-tray

Thin roots of herbaceous plants such as perennial phloxes can be encouraged to root by cutting them into 2.5–3.6cm/1–1½in-long pieces and placing flat on a mixture of equal parts moist peat and sharp sand, with a dusting of sand on top.

These cuttings are removed from the plant during its dormant period, preferably in late winter or early spring. Sieve a 6–12mm/¼–½in layer of compost over them, then place in a cold frame. When shoots appear and roots have formed, pot up plants or place in a nurserybed.

The Drumstick Primula (Primula denticulata) *can be increased in the same way.*

BORDER CARNATIONS *can be layered during early and mid-summer. Select a young, vigorous, healthy shoot from the outside of a plant and use a sharp knife to form a tongue just below the leaves and a leaf joint, and on the side away from the parent plant. At this stage, the shoot is still attached to the plant.*

DUST *the stem with hormone rooting-powder, then peg it 3.6–5cm/1½–2in deep in moist, friable soil; tongues open.*

AFTER *about two months, roots will have developed from the tongue. Sever the stem close to the parent plant, as well as next to the rooted part. Pot up the young plant.*

DAHLIAS &
CHRYSANTHEMUMS

❖

Dahlias are richly coloured, tender, tuberous-rooted plants that are soon damaged by frosts. Therefore, in late spring or early summer of each year (as soon as all risk of frost has passed) newly raised plants are put into borders. Alternatively, the previous year's tubers can be divided and replanted.

Growing dahlias is easy and their needs are quite simple; plenty of sun, moisture and food. In part, these are

DIVIDING TUBERS *is an easy way to increase dahlias. Lift the tubers in autumn, cut down and store in a frost-proof shed or greenhouse, then divide in spring, ensuring that each part has at least one healthy eye (bud). Dust cut surfaces with a fungicide.*

necessary because dahlias come from sunny Mexico, but mainly because within the span of a few months they grow from cuttings to plants often 1.5m/5ft high.

RANGE OF DAHLIAS
There are several types and they are classified according to their vigour as well as the shape and

size of their flowers. The basic classifications for them are Bedding Dahlias and Border Dahlias.

• Bedding Dahlias are used to create a carpet of colour at or below knee height, and are normally raised from seeds sown in late winter or early spring.

• Border Dahlias form the larger group and include several types, all raised from cuttings or by division.

They include Single-flowered, Anemone-flowered, Collerette and Paeony-flowered types, as well as Decoratives which range from 75cm/2½ft to 1.5m/5ft tall and with varying flower sizes. Pompon types at about 90cm/3ft high are superb, while Cactus-like types include plants from 90cm–1.5m/ 3–5ft high with a range of various flower sizes.

1. AS SOON *as frost blackens the leaves of dahlias, shorten back the stems and use a garden fork to dig under the tubers to lift them out of the soil. Take care not to spike the tubers with the fork.*

2. CUT *the stems to about 15cm/6in long, remove soil from around the tubers and leave them upside down in a shed or under a bench in a cool greenhouse for a couple of weeks. Ensure the area is vermin proof.*

3. PUT *the tubers into 10–13cm/4–5in-deep boxes. Pack slightly damp peat around and lightly over them, but do not cover their crowns. Place the boxes in an airy shed, at 5°C/41°F during winter.*

To the purist who would grow only herbaceous perennials in a border, dahlias are taboo. But for bringing additional colour to borders, the dahlia has few peers.

CHRYSANTHEMUMS FOR HERBACEOUS BORDERS

The chrysanthemum family is formed of several types: annuals, those with an alpine nature, hardy perennials, and a wide group of half-hardy types which have become known as florists' chrysanthemums. These can be grown outdoors in herbaceous borders, where they are planted in late spring or early summer each year, when risk of frost has passed.

They are best planted in bold groups, in spaces specially left for them in borders. Fresh plants are raised each year from cuttings which have been developed from the previous year's plants.

In late autumn, pack cut-down chrysanthemum plants (stools) into boxes of compost. Place in a cold frame or light, cool shed and in late winter water and place in gentle warmth. Shoots will appear and these can also be used to form cuttings.

1. IN LATE *winter, chrysanthemum roots (stools) that were cut down and boxed up in late autumn and placed in a cold frame or cool shed can be encouraged to develop shoots.*

2. CUT OFF *healthy shoots and trim below a leaf joint to 5–6cm/ 2–2½in long. Remove the lower leaves and dip their bases in hormone rooting-powder.*

3. FILL *and firm compost in a small pot and insert three or four cuttings about 18–25mm/³/4–1in deep and 12mm/½in from the pot's side. Firm compost, water lightly and place in gentle warmth.*

4. IN LATE *winter, re-pack the tubers into boxes of compost; water and place them in 15–18°C/59–64°. Sever shoots when 7.5cm/ 3in long; cut off the lower leaves and trim them beneath a leaf joint.*

5. INSERT *cuttings 2.5cm/1in deep in pots of equal parts moist peat and sharp sand. Several cuttings can be put in a 7.5cm/3in-wide pot, at least 12mm/ ½in from the side. Place in 15–18°C/59–64°.*

6. WHEN *rooted, pot them into individual pots filled with a general potting compost. Take care not to damage the roots. Water the compost well and when established reduce the temperature slightly.*

PLANNING & PLANTING

❖

LANT herbaceous borders in early to mid-autumn, or during mid-spring. However, in mild areas, planting could continue from autumn until early winter, or start in early spring. Where new borders have been dug in winter, spring is the better time as the soil will have settled and the surface be broken down to a fine tilth. However, early flowering plants are best planted in autumn (see page 16 for the best times to divide established plants).

PREPARING THE BORDER

Do not try to plant herbaceous plants too early in spring as, if the soil is excessively wet, their soft crowns will decay. Also, cold soil prevents rapid establishment.

As soon as the surface soil is dry, systematically shuffle sideways across the bed, firming strips 25–30cm/10–12in wide at a time. This is time consuming, but better than using a garden roller. After firming, rake the surface level. The 'plan' (see opposite page) can then be transferred to it.

PLANTING

Setting plants in the soil is a critical task; if positioned too deeply in cold, wet clay soil they may decay. Conversely, if planted shallowly in light soil that settles, their exposed crowns may become hard and the entire plant will be rocked, or topple over. Always put plants with long tap roots slightly deeper (about 2.5cm/1in) than before: these include acanthus, anchusas, Oriental Poppies and verbascums. The previous soil level is usually indicated by a dirty mark on each plant's crown.

Plants with fibrous roots, such as *Achillea ptarmica*, Michaelmas Daisies, phloxes and pyrethrums, must not be planted deeply, and this especially applies to surface-rooting plants such as London Pride, monardas and Lamb's Tongue *(Stachys byzantina)*.

Whatever the depth, firm planting is essential. Use the heel of your shoe to firm in large plants, and your hands for smaller ones. Afterwards, ensure that the soil is watered thoroughly.

1. PLAN *the border carefully (see opposite page), preferably setting plants in groups of three. Before planting, lay the plants on the soil to ensure that each group is in proportion with itself and neighbouring plants.*

2. USE *a trowel to form a deep hole so that roots are allowed to spread out and not become congested towards one side. Bury the crown slightly deeper than before: this allows for the soil to settle slightly after planting.*

3. FIRM SOIL *around the plants, using your fingers. If the soil is too heavily compressed, air is excluded and plants suffer. Conversely, if the soil is not in close contact with the roots, establishment is delayed.*

MAKING YOUR PLAN

Detailed planning is essential if an herbaceous border, when in flower, is to look natural and in harmony with itself. Height variations, colour harmonies and contrast need consideration, as well as the planting practicalities of 'how many plants will I need?'

For this reason, both the heights of the mature plants and their planting distances are indicated for each of the plants illustrated from pages 26 to 55.

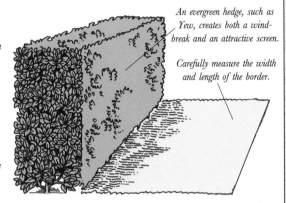

1. FIRST, *measure the width and length of the border. If you do not have a long tape-measure, tie knots every metre or yard in a long piece of string. Do not walk on the border too much, as this soon consolidates the soil unevenly.*

An evergreen hedge, such as Yew, creates both a wind-break and an attractive screen.

Carefully measure the width and length of the border.

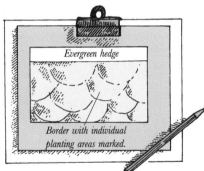

Evergreen hedge

Border with individual planting areas marked.

2. TRANSFER *the measurements onto scaled paper. Then, draw in the planting areas. The size of these depend on the planting distances: borders look best when plants are grouped in threes and planted in triangles. As an approximation, the space needed for each group is about twice the planting width indicated (in the following pages) for each plant.*

3. TRANSFER *the design to the border, using a pointed stick to define the areas. Alternatively, use a thin trickle of sharp sand. Do not use lime, as this may make the area too alkaline. The planting areas invariably increase in size towards the back – or centre, if an island border – to accommodate larger and more dominant herbaceous perennials.*

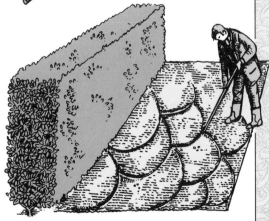

LOOKING AFTER HERBACEOUS PLANTS

❖

BECAUSE herbaceous perennials develop fresh stems, leaves and flowers each year, it is vital that ample food and water are available to enable plants to grow healthily and vigorously throughout summer.

The first task in spring is to shallowly fork the soil between established plants, removing weeds and opening up the surface so that air and water can enter. Then, sprinkle a general fertilizer around plants and thoroughly water the soil. At this stage, in late spring or early summer, form a 5–7.5cm/2–3in-thick mulch of well-decayed compost between plants. There are many other mulches that can be used, including chopped bark. Peat has been used in the past, but its removal from peat beds is environmentally unfriendly. Also, birds usually scattered it over lawns and paths. Before applying any mulch, ensure the soil is moist.

AUTUMN OR SPRING?

Most gardeners cut down their herbaceous perennials in autumn, after their display is completely finished. This tidies up a border and ensures that pests and diseases on old stems and leaves can be destroyed by burning. Twiggy sticks, canes and proprietary supports can be removed and stored under cover during winter, but first remove soil from them and, if necessary, wash in disinfectant so that plants during the following year are not contaminated with problems carried over from the previous season.

Occasionally, however, plants are left in position during winter. The idea is that frost on the old stems creates an interesting feature during the cold weather. If plants are treated in this way, cut them back in late winter, then remove their supports and rake off and burn all debris from the surface. This means that late winter can become a very busy time.

IN EARLY *spring, re-firm herbaceous perennials planted in autumn. The soil may have been loosened by frost. It is essential that roots and soil are in close contact if the plants are to grow quickly.*

DURING *spring and early summer, shallowly fork between plants, breaking up crusty surface soil to enable air and rain to penetrate. At the same time, pull up and remove all weeds.*

IN LATE *spring or early summer, sprinkle a general fertilizer between the plants. Then, lightly hoe it in to the topsoil. Take care not to damage roots. Thoroughly water the bed.*

STAKING

Many herbaceous perennials do not need staking (see pages 30 and 31). However, some, such as paeonies, dahlias and delphiniums benefit from supports that eventually become covered by stems, leaves and flowers.

Three stout stakes, encircled by strong garden string at several heights. This is an excellent to way to support border dahlias.

Twiggy pea-sticks are ideal for most plants: insert them early in the season, so that shoots grow up and completely cloak them.

Curved, metal supports are ideal for supporting paeonies, as the stems can rest on the circular metal sides.

DEAD-HEADING PLANTS

Removing dead flower heads is time consuming, but certainly prolongs the display. In a large border this may not be important, but in small town gardens it is a useful activity.

Instead of just dropping spent flowers on the soil, put them on a compost heap.

FEEDING

Start the yearly cycle of feeding in spring (see opposite page), then add a mulch to the soil's surface.

If the border has not been mulched, general fertilizers applied in a granular form are ideal, lightly pricked into the surface and then thoroughly watered. Apply these every three weeks until the latter part of mid-summer. If a mulch is present, use a liquid feed.

Take care not to over feed lupins, eryngiums, artemisias, echinops and anaphalis as they may then produce rank and leafy growth, which is unattractive and susceptible to pests and disease attack. Many plants with silver or grey leaves are soon spoiled when fed too often. They are better when they are 'hungry'.

FORM *a 5–7.5cm/ 2–3in-thick layer of well-decomposed compost between plants in late spring or early summer, but first apply a general fertilizer and thoroughly water the soil.*

THROUGHOUT *summer, water the plants. Oscillating sprays make this task easier and do a superb job. Always apply water thoroughly, not just superficially dampening the surface.*

IN AUTUMN, *cut down plants to ground level and rake debris from the surface. This is woody and needs to be burned. Sometimes cutting down plants is left until late winter.*

TALL PLANTS

❖

E XTRA-tall plants are ideal for creating both focal points and height variations in borders. Some, such as Michaelmas Daisy *(Aster novae-angiae)*, produce a spectacle of massed flowers, while the Globe Artichoke *(Cynara scolymus)* has fewer but more unusually-shaped flower heads. Alternatively, the Ornamental Rhubarb *(Rheum palmatum)* has dominant foliage.

Where a garden is exposed to strong and constant winds, ensure tall plants are either staked or protected by screens or hedges. Tall hedges that filter wind are the long-term answer to the problem. Indeed, traditional double-sided herbaceous borders were often backed by Yew hedges. As well as giving protection, they provided an attractive backdrop.

OTHER TALL PLANTS

- Acanthus mollis
- Acanthus spinosus
- Achillea filipendulina
- Aster novae-angliae
- Aruncus dioicus
- Campanula lactiflora
- Crambe cordifolia
- Delphinium elatum
- Echinacea purpurea
- Eremurus robustus
- Eremurus 'Shelford Hybrids'
- Ligularia dentata
- Macleaya cordata
- Onopordum acanthium
- Rudbeckia laciniata
- Verbascum bombyciferum (V. 'Broussa')

ASTER NOVI-BELGII
*(Michaelmas Daisy)
normally grows 90cm–
1.2m/3–4ft high, but there
are dwarf forms 23–38cm/
9–15in tall. They bloom
during late summer and into
autumn, with large, daisy-
like flowers. Colours include
blue, red, pink, purple and
white. Plant 23–38cm/
9–15in apart.*

ACONITUM NAPELLUS
*(Monkshood/Helmet Flower)
grows 90cm–1.2m/3–4ft
high, with deeply cut leaves
and spires of hooded flowers
during mid and late summer.
Colours include many tones
of blue and violet, as well
as ivory-white. They are
distinctive and create a
superb display. Plant them
30–38cm/12–15in apart.*

CYNARA SCOLYMUS
*(Globe Artichoke) grows
about 1.5m/5ft high.
It is mainly grown for its
edible flower heads, but is
sufficiently decorative to be
planted in a border. The
purplish blue flowers appear
during mid to late summer.
Space plants 90cm/3ft
apart. Protect the bases
of plants in winter.*

EREMURUS ELWESII
(Foxtail Lily/Desert Candle/King's Spear) grows 1.8–2.7m/6–9ft high and develops fragrant, soft pink flowers in thick, poker-like heads during early and into mid-summer. There is also 'Albus', a white-flowered variety. Space plants 60–90cm/2–3ft apart.

GALEGA OFFICINALIS
(Goat's Rue) grows up to 1.5m/5ft high and during early and mid-summer develops white or pale lilac flowers amid light green leaves formed of many small leaflets. 'Alba' is a pure white variety. Space plants 60–75cm/2–2½ft apart. Ideal for backs of borders.

HELENIUM AUTUMNALE
(Sneezeweed) reaches 1.2–1.8m/4–6ft high and develops large, daisy-like flowers from mid-summer to autumn. Some varieties are 60–75cm/2–2½ft high. Flower colours range from yellow, through orange to mahogany red. Space plants 30–45cm/1–1½ft apart.

HELIANTHUS DECAPETALUS *(Thin-leaf Sunflower) has rough, green leaves and 5–7.5cm/2–3in-wide yellow flowers from mid to late summer. The best known varieties include 'Capenoch Star' (lemon yellow) and 'Loddon Gold' (golden yellow). Space these handsome plants 45–60cm/1½–2ft apart.*

RHEUM PALMATUM *(Ornamental Rhubarb) is 1.5–2.4m/5–8ft tall, with large, deeply cut, purple-red leaves that slowly lose their dominant colour. Tall, deep pink or red flowers appear in early and mid-summer. 'Atropurpureum' has purple-tinged leaves and creamy white flowers. Space plants 90cm/3ft apart.*

THALICTRUM DIPTEROCARPUM *(Meadow Rue) grows 1.2–1.5m/4–5ft high, with small mauve flowers and dominant yellow anthers from early to mid-summer. It is sometimes sold as T. delavayi. Varieties include 'Hewitt's Double' (double and mauve). Space plants 45cm/18in apart.*

27

LOW-GROWING PLANTS
❖

LARGE, distinctively-shaped, dominant plants always attract attention, but in small gardens are often overpowering, especially when seen *en masse* and close up. There are, however, many small plants to choose from and a few are illustrated and listed here.

Many of them act as ground covers and smother soil in leaves and flowers (further examples of these are discussed on pages 32 and 33). Others have a more upright nature, some combining attractive leaves with flowers. Lamb's Tongue (now called *Stachys byzantina* but earlier and more popularly known as *S. lanata* and *S. olympica*) is a superb example of a foliage plant for borders, whatever their size.

> #### KEEPING DOGS QUIET
>
> *During the sixteenth century the barber-surgeon and herbalist John Gerard said that* Cynoglossum offinale *prevented dogs barking at you.*

Any list of low-growing plants raises the question 'what exactly is low?' Ground-covering plants are discussed on pages 32 and 33. They tend to be shorter than the low-growing ones featured here which all have a maximum height of about 60cm/2ft. These heights include flowers and therefore many plants appear less dominant when not in bloom.

CYNOGLOSSUM NERVOSUM *(Hound's Tongue/Beggar's Lice) grows 45–60cm/1¹/2–2ft high, with rough, grey-green, tongue-like leaves. Vivid blue, tubular, Forget-me-not-like flowers are borne on branching stems during early and mid-summer. Position the plants 30cm/12in apart.*

LYCHNIS x ARKWRIGHTII *grows about 30cm/12in high and produces lance-shaped, mahogany-shaded leaves. Brilliant scarlet-vermilion flowers, about 36mm/1¹/2in wide, appear from early to mid-summer – sometimes slightly later. Set the plants 23–30cm/9–12in apart.*

EUPHORBIA POLYCHROMA *(*E. epithymoides*) is a bushy, shrubby, evergreen perennial about 45cm/18in high. The fresh green foliage is attractive, with wide clusters of sulphur yellow bracts during late spring and early summer. Space plants 45cm/1¹/2ft apart.*

POLYGONUM AFFINE *(Knotweed) forms mats of lance-shaped leaves. 'Darjeeling Red' has deep pink flowers from mid to late summer; 'Donald Lowndes' has red flowers and copper-coloured leaves in autumn. Both grow 15–25cm/ 6–10in high. Set the plants 30–18cm/ 12–15in apart.*

POTENTILLA ATROSANGUINEA *(Cinquefoil) is a parent of many superb herbaceous perennials, most growing 38–60cm/ 15–24in high. These include 'Gibson's Scarlet' (brilliant scarlet) and 'Wm Rollison' (rich orange). Set plants 38–45cm/ 15–18in apart.*

PRUNELLA GRANDIFLORA *(Self-heal) grows 15cm/ 6in high, with purple-violet flowers from early summer to autumn. P. x webbiana is slightly larger; several varieties, including 'Loveliness' (pale violet) and 'Loveliness Pink' (clear pink). Space plants 38cm/ 15in apart.*

FURTHER PLANTS

- Ajuga reptans *(10–30cm/ 4–12in)*
- Alchemilla mollis *(30–45cm/ 12–18in)*
- Armeria maritima *(15–25cm/ 6–10in)*
- Aster novi-belgii *(dwarf varieties – 23–45cm/ 9–18in)*
- Bergenia cordifolia *(30cm/ 12in)*
- Brunnera macrophylla *30–45cm/ 12–18in)*
- Corydalis lutea *(15–25cm/ 6–10in)*
- Dicentra eximia *(30–45cm/ 12–18in)*
- Epimedium *species (23–30cm/ 9–12in)*
- Geranium endressii *(30–45cm/ 12–18in*
- Geum x borisii *(30cm/ 12in high)*
- Heuchera sanguineum *(30–45cm/ 12–18in)*
- Hosta albo-marginata *(38–45cm/ 15–18in)*
- Limonium latifolium *(45–60cm/ 18–24in)*
- Saxifraga umbrosa *(30cm/ 12in)*
- Stachys byzantina *(30–45cm/ 12–18in)*

(Note: The measurements indicate their heights)

SEDUM SPECTABILE *(Ice Plant) is 30–45cm/ 12–18in high, with fleshy, whitish-green leaves. Pink flowers appear in clustered heads during late summer and into autumn. 'Autumn Joy' has large, bright rose-salmon flowers that assume bronze tinges. Set the plants 45cm/ 18in apart.*

PLANTS THAT
DO NOT NEED STAKING

❖

A T ONE time it was assumed that all herbaceous plants had to be supported, and they were automatically planted in long borders backed by a hedge. Since the 1950s, however, self-supporting herbaceous plants have been increasingly used in borders that form islands in lawns (see page 11). This meant that the frontal lengths of borders increased dramatically and more low, self-supporting plants were needed. This does not mean that all tall plants – staked or self-supporting – should be omitted from borders, as they create variations in height.

Self-supporting herbaceous plants are a boon in small gardens, especially where space is limited for the storage of stakes throughout winter. Also, in town gardens it is often difficult to obtain twiggy supports.

ANEMONE x HYBRIDA
(Japanese Anemone) grows
60–90cm/2–3ft high and
develops flowers up to
7.5cm/3in wide from mid-
summer to the frosts of
autumn. There are several
varieties, mainly in white
or pink. Space plants 30–
38cm/12–15in apart.

CURTONUS
PANICULATUS (Aunt
Eliza/Pleated Leaves)
develops from corms and
eventually creates a large
clump. It grows 90cm–
1.2m/3–4ft high and bears
deep orange-red flowers in
mid and late summer. Space
plants 23cm/9in apart.

CAMASSIA QUAMASH
(Common Camosh/
Quamash), also known as
C. esculenta, grows 60–
75cm/2–2½ft high and
bears white, purple or blue
flowers in early and mid-
summer. C. leichtlinii is
slightly taller. Space plants
about 15cm/6in apart.

INULA HELENIUM
(Elecampane) grows
90cm–1.2m/3–4ft high and
produces large, bright yellow,
daisy-like flowers during mid
and late summer. Other
species include I. royleana
and I. hookeri. Set these
plants about 38–45cm/
15–18in apart.

OTHER
PLANTS

- *Acanthus*
- *Achillea*
- *Aconitum*
- *Agapanthus*
- *Alchemilla*
- *Anaphalis*
- *Armeria*
- *Astilbe*
- *Astrantia*
- *Bergenia*
- *Catananche*
- *Centaurea*
- *Crocosmia*
- *Dicentra*
- *Dictamnus*
- *Doronicum*
- *Echinacea*
- *Echinops*
- *Eremurus*
- *Eupatorum*
- *Euphorbia*
- *Helenium*
- *Helleborus*
- *Hemerocallis*
- *Heuchera*
- *Hosta*
- *Iris*
- *Kniphofia*
- *Limonium*
- *Lupinus*
- *Lychnis*
- *Lysimachia*
- *Lythrum*
- *Monarda*
- *Oenothera*
- *Onopordum*
- *Phlomis*
- *Pulmonaria*
- *Rudbeckia*
- *Scabiosa*
- *Sedum*
- *Sisyrinchium*
- *Stachys*
- *Trillium*
- *Trollius*
- *Verbascum*
- *Zantedeschia*

MERTENSIA VIRGINICA
*(Virginian Cowslip/
Roanoke-bells)* grows
30–60cm/1–2ft high and
has purple-blue flowers
during late spring and early
summer. From mid-summer
onwards, plants die down
completely. Space plants
25–30cm/10–12in apart.

PHYTOLACCA
AMERICANA *(Poke Weed/
Red-ink Plant)* grows 90cm–
1.8m/3–6ft high and develops spikes of white flowers
from early summer to early
autumn, followed by dark
purple berries containing a
dark red juice. Space plants
90cm/3ft apart.

PHALARIS
ARUNDINACEA *'Picta'
(Gardener's Garters)* is a
perennial ornamental grass
with narrow, tapering leaves
variegated cream and bright
green. It grows 30–45cm/
12–18in high and initially
is planted 38–45cm/
15–18in apart. But it soon
forms a large clump. Replant
it every two or three years.

POLYGONATUM x
HYBRIDUM *(Solomon's
Seal/David's Harp)* grows
60–75cm/2–2½ft high and
develops white flowers up to
2.5cm/1in long in clusters
of two or three during early
summer. Space plants
30–38cm/12–15in apart.
It is ideal for planting in
light shade, although it grows
practically anywhere.

GROUND COVER PLANTS

❖

SMOTHERING soil with leaves is an ideal way to prevent the growth of weeds and to create a handsome backdrop for other plants. Many low-growing plants can be used and a few of them are suggested here.

Some plants flourish in shade and these are especially useful, but do not expect them to develop to their full size when light is scarce and there is a dearth of moisture.

Establishing herbaceous ground-covering plants in shade is sometimes difficult, but planting them in spring and ensuring their roots remain moist throughout the first season assists them. Unfortunately, the added moisture attracts slugs and snails. Regularly inspect leaves and check under plants.

OTHER PLANTS

- Ajuga reptans 'Atropurpurea'
- Bergenia cordifolia
- Brunnera macrophylla
- Epimedium perralderianum
- Epimedium pinnatum
- Geranium endressii
- Geranium grandiflorum
- Heuchera sanguinea
- Heucherella tiarelloides
- Lysimachia nummularia
- Nepeta x faassenii
- Polygonum affine
- Pulmonaria officinalis
- Stachys byzantina
- Tellima grandiflora

DRYAS OCTOPETALA *(Mountain Avens) grows 7.5–10cm/3–4in high and creates a mat of deep green leaves. White, saucer-shaped flowers appear during early and mid-summer. Space plants 45cm/18in apart.*

HOSTA FORTUNEI *'Albopicta' (Plantain Lily) grows about 45cm/18in high and displays pale green leaves variegated buff yellow. Space these ground-smothering plants 45cm/18in apart.*

LAMIUM GALEOBDOLON *'Variegatum' (Variegated Yellow Archangel) grows 15–38cm/6–15in high, with silver flushed leaves and yellow flowers in early and mid-summer. Space plants 38cm/15in apart.*

PULMONARIA SACCHARATA *(Bethlehem Sage/Lungwort) grows 30cm/12in high and has leaves spotted silvery-white. Pink flowers that slowly change to sky blue appear during spring. Space the plants 30cm/12in apart.*

TOLMIEA MENZIESII *(Pig-a-Back/Youth on Age) grows about 15cm/6in high and covers the ground with Maple-like leaves. Greenish white flowers appear during early summer. It is ideal in partial shade. Space plants 30–38cm/12–15in apart.*

SAXIFRAGA UMBROSA *(London Pride) forms masses of rosettes that carpet soil. Masses of pink, star-shaped flowers appear in clusters on stems about 20cm/8in high during late spring and early summer. Space plants 30cm/12in apart.*

VERONICA GENTIANOIDES *grows 23–38cm/9–15in high and smothers borders with leafy rosettes. Blue flowers borne in terminal clusters up to 15cm/6in long appear in early summer. The form 'Variegata' has creamy white leaves.*

TIARELLA WHERRYI *(False Mitrewort) grows 15–30cm/6–12in high, with ivy-shaped, pale green leaves. Creamy white flowers appear throughout summer. T. cordifolia (Foam Flower) is another superb ground-covering species.*

GOD'S IMPRINT

Many early herbalists believed that 'God hath imprinted upon the Plants, Herbs and Flowers, as it were Hieroglyphicks, the signature of their Vertues'. *For this reason,* Pulmonaria officinalis *with its white-spotted leaves was thought to cure diseased lungs. It is also known as Blue Lungwort, Jerusalem Cowslip and, amusingly, as Spotted Dog.*

WINDY & EXPOSED SITES
❖

STRONG winds make it very difficult to establish plants: they are either blown about or desiccated by drying winds. Temporary screens help to encourage young plants to become established, while watering and mulching the soil, as well as re-firming loose soil around plants in spring, encourages their development. The plants suggested here will thrive once established, but even they will not grow on a bleak, windswept mountain.

When establishing an exposed garden, first plant windbreaks and hedges to filter wind to reduce its strength. Brick walls create plant-damaging swirling winds on their lee sides and therefore stout hedges are better. Alternatively, temporary screens of hessian provide shelter.

OTHER PLANTS

- Alchemilla mollis
- Anaphalis triplinervis
- Anemone *x* hybrida
- Asters (short types)
- Centaurea dealbata
- Coreopsis grandiflora
- Dictamnus albus
- Eryngium maritimum
- Geranium endressii
- Geranium grandiflorum
- Gysophila paniculata
- Polygonum affine
- Potentilla – *hybrids of* P. atrosanguinea
- Rudbeckia hirta – *low-growing* varieties
- Scabiosa caucasica
- Sedum spectabile
- Veronica spicata

CHELONE OBLIQUA *(Turtlehead/Snakehead) grows 45–60cm/1¹/₂–2ft high and during mid and late summer develops terminal clusters of deep rose, snapdragon-like flowers on stiff, upright stems. Space the plants 30–45cm/12–18in apart.*

HEUCHERA SANGUINEA *(Coral Flower/Coral Bells) grows 30–45cm/ 12–18in high and produces masses of slender stems bearing wispy, bright red, bell-shaped flowers throughout summer. The round or heart-shaped leaves carpet the ground. Space plants 38cm/15in apart.*

LIATRIS SPICATA *(Blazing Star/Gay Feather) grows 60–75cm/ 2–2¹/₂ft high and during late summer develops wand-like spires of pink-purple flowers. Space plants 38cm/15in apart.*

PROTECTING PLANTS

The importance of preventing extremely cold winds damaging newly planted herbaceous plants, trees and shrubs has been known for centuries. Screens have been created from two layers of wire-netting with straw between them. In the early 1800s the garden writer John Loudon recommended straw tied in rolls and strung together.

PLATYCODON GRANDI-FLORUM *(Balloon Flower) grows 30–60cm/ 1–2ft high and develops balloon-shaped flower buds. These open throughout summer and reveal light blue, saucer-shaped flowers. The form 'Album' has white flowers. Space plants about 38cm/ 15in apart.*

LYCHNIS CORONARIA *(Rose Campion/Mullien Pink) grows about 45cm/ 18in high and displays a wealth of bright, crimson-magenta flowers from mid to late summer. It is a short-lived perennial. Space plants 23–30cm/ 9–12in apart.*

OENOTHERA MISSOURIENSIS *(Evening Primrose) grows 10–15cm/ 4–6in high and creates a mass of yellow flowers up to 7.5cm/ 3in wide during summer. They open in the evening and each flower lasts for several days. Space plants 38cm/ 15in apart.*

SCABIOSA CAUCASICA *(Caucasian Scabious/ Sweet Scabious) grows 45–60cm/ 1½–2ft high, with low clusters of leaves and lavender-blue flowers about 7.5cm/ 3in wide on long stems from early to late summer. There are several varieties, in white, blue and purple. Space plants 38cm/ 15in apart.*

STOKESIA LAEVIS *(Stokes' Aster) grows 30–45cm/ 12–18in high and bears white, lilac, blue or purple flowers up to 7.5cm/ 3in wide during mid and late summer and into autumn. Space the plants about 38cm/ 15in apart.*

DRY & SUNNY POSITIONS

❖

Hot, dry, sunny borders make growing herbaceous plants difficult. But there are some plants that tolerate these conditions and, once established, thrive. Some of them are described here.

Do not leave the establishment of these plants to chance as, even though they survive in dry borders, plenty of well-decayed compost mixed with the soil assists them during their early years. Additionally, covering the soil with a mulch reduces moisture loss from the surface. Until the plants are established cover the ground with leaves and stems. Before applying a mulch, always thoroughly water the soil.

Many Mediterranean plants survive in dry places, especially those with silver or white leaves.

KING'S SPEAR

Asphodelus is, undeservedly, less popular today than a century or so ago. The species Asphodelus luteus *was known to William Turner, the father of English botany, during the early 1500s, but is now properly called* Asphodeline lutea, *the King's Spear. It grows about 1.2m/4ft high and develops stiff spikes of sulphur yellow flowers.*

The Greeks ate roots of asphodelus and during the Middle Ages it was known as Cibo Regia, *food for a king. The Greeks often planted asphodelus around tombs to provide nourishment for spirits.*

ACHILLEA MILLEFOLIUM
(Yarrow/Sanguinary/Nosebleed) grows about 60cm/ 2ft high and develops white to cerise flowers in large, flattened heads from early to late summer. Space the plants 30–38cm/12–15in apart. Varieties include 'Cerise Queen' with cherry red flowers.

ARTEMISIA LUDOVICIANA *(White Sage/Cudweed) is a North American native and grows 60cm–1.2m/2–4ft high. It is mainly grown for its white, woolly leaves. Plant it about 38cm/15in apart. Other herbaceous types include A. lactiflora (White Mugwort), with deeply cut and lobed, mid-green leaves.*

BAPTISIA AUSTRALIS *(False Indigo/Blue False Indigo) grows 60cm–1.2m/ 2–4ft high and develops masses of blue, sweet-pea-like flowers during early summer. This North American plant sometimes takes a couple of seasons to become fully established. Space these magnificent plants 45– 60cm/1/2–2ft apart.*

BUPHTHALMUM SALICIFOLIUM *(Willow-leaf Ox-eye) grows up to 75cm/2¹⁄₂ft high when left to form a tumbling bush. Bright, golden yellow, daisy-like flowers appear from early summer to autumn. The leaves are slightly hairy. Space the plants about 45cm/18in apart.*

MACLEAYA CORDATA *(Plume Poppy/Tree Celandine) grows up to 2.4m/8ft high and creates 90cm/3ft-long spires packed with small, pearly white flowers during summer. The lower leaves are large and deeply lobed. It is ideal for the back of a border. Position the plants 90cm/3ft apart.*

SOLIDAGO *'Goldenmosa' (Golden Rod) is a garden hybrid that grows 75–90cm/2¹⁄₂–3ft high and develops 15–23cm/6–9in-long sprays of fluffy yellow flowers during mid and into late summer. Space plants 38cm/15in apart. There are many other hybrids to choose from.*

HELIOPSIS SCABRA *(Orange Sunflower/Ox-eye), also known as H. helianthoides scabra, grows 90cm–1.2m/3–4ft high and develops single, daisy-like yellow flowers in mid and late summer. Varieties include 'Golden Plume'. Space plants 45–60cm/1¹⁄₂–2ft apart.*

NEPETA x FAASSENII *(Catmint) is a hybrid that grows 30–45cm/12–18in high and develops whorls of lavender blue flowers throughout summer. When planted in a group it is ideal for covering large areas. Space the plants about 30cm/12in apart. Cats are fascinated by it.*

OTHER PLANTS

- Anaphalis triplinervis
- Anthemis *spp.*
- Asphodeline lutea
- Catananche caerulea
- Centaurea dealbata
- Centaurea macrocephala
- Echinops ritro
- Eryngium *spp.*
- Gypsophila paniculata
- Limonium latifolium
- Sedum *spp.*
- Stachys byzantina

SHADY POSITIONS

❖

EW gardens are not partially shaded during some part of the day and most plants, whatever their nature, tolerate this. Occasionally, however, neighbouring trees or buildings cast shade throughout the day. This is when shade-loving plants are needed.

ADAPTABLE PLANTS

All plants need sunlight to activate growth and to keep them healthy, but some have evolved to live under trees and therefore happily survive in shade. Although trees deprive plants growing underneath them of total light, they do provide shelter from cold winds, frosts and strong sunlight. Shade from evergreen trees and shrubs may be too dense and continuous for many plants, but deciduous trees allow more light to reach plants in winter, as well as sheltering them from late spring frosts. Most herbaceous plants, of course, are not able to benefit from extra light in winter, but deciduous trees enable more rain to reach plants than would evergreens.

<u>PLANTS FOR</u>
<u>DRY SHADE</u>

- Anaphalus margaritacea
- Anaphalus triplinervis
- Crambe cordifolia
- Epimedium *x* rubrum
- Geranium ibericum
- Polygonum affine

AJUGA REPTANS
*(Bugle/ Carpet Bugleweed)
grows 10–30cm/ 4–12in
high. Blue flowers in early
and mid-summer. Space
plants 38cm/ 15in apart.*

DICENTRA SPECTABILIS
*(Bleeding Heart) grows 45–
75cm/ 1½–2½ft high. Rosy
red, heart-shaped flowers in
early summer. Space plants
38cm/ 15in apart.*

HEMEROCALLIS
HYBRIDS *(Day Lilies) are
60–90cm/ 2–3ft high and
develop flowers in yellow,
pink, red or ruby-purple in
early and mid-summer. Space
plants 45cm/ 18in apart.*

LYSICHITON
AMERICANUS *(Skunk
Cabbage) grows 60–90cm/
2–3ft high, with yellow
flowers in late spring. Choose
a moist and shady position.*

LYTHRUM SALICARIA
(Purple Loosestrife/ Spiked Loosestrife) grows 60cm– 1.2m/ 2–4ft high and from early to late summer reveals small, reddish purple flowers in spires up to 25cm/ 10in long. Space plants 38– 45cm/ 15–18in apart.

PELTIPHYLLUM PELTATUM *(Umbrella Plant) grows about 1m/ 3¹/₂ft high and displays pink flowers in parasol-like heads during late spring and early summer. Large leaves appear later. Space plants 90cm/ 3ft apart.*

PULMONARIA OFFICINALIS *(Jerusalem Cowslip/ Spotted Dog) grows 30cm/ 12in high and develops narrow oval green leaves with white spots. It flowers in late spring and early summer. Space plants 30cm/ 12in apart.*

SMILACINA RACEMOSA
(False Spikenard/ Treacleberry) grows 75–90cm/ 2¹/₂–3ft high. During late spring and early summer it bears creamy white, scented flowers. It is ideal for shady, moist areas. Space plants 38cm/ 15in apart. The Star-flowered Lily-of-the-Valley (S. stellata) has star-shaped white flowers.

PLANTS FOR DEEP SHADE AND MOISTURE-RETENTIVE SOIL

- Aruncus dioicus *(Goat's Beard)*
- Astilbe *x* arendsii *(Perennial Spiraea)*
- Cimicifuga racemosa *(Black Snake Root)*
- Epimedium perralderianum *(Bishop's Hat/ Barren Wort)*
- Helleborus foetidus *(Stinking Hellebore)*
- Helleborus niger *(Christmas Rose)*
- Helleborus orientalis *(Lenten Rose)*
- Polygonatum commutatum *(Giant Solomon's Seal)*
- Polygonatum *x* hybridum *(Solomon's Seal/ David's Harp)*
- Tiarella cordifolia *(Foam Flower)*
- Trillium grandiflorum *(Wake Robin)*
- Trillium undulatum *(Painted Wood-lily)*

Wake Robin (Trillium grandiflorum) *has flowers that are at first white, then later flushed with rose-pink.*

39

MOIST POSITIONS

❖

Many herbaceous plants thrive in moist soils, especially those that are fertile and therefore able to encourage rapid growth. This is essential with plants that each year grow from a dormant rootstock.

In addition to the plants featured here, many primulas are ideal for planting in soil that does not dry out in summer, perhaps in a bed alongside a garden pond. These include *Primula beesiana* (lilac-purple), *P. bulleyana* (light orange), *P. denticulata* (Drumstick Primrose; pale lilac, deep purple, rose, deep carmine or white), *P. florindae* (Giant Cowslip; light orange to blood red) and *P. japonica* (Japanese Primrose; magenta-red, but also white and pink).

OTHER PLANTS

- Astilbe *x* arendsii
- Gunnera manicata
- Hemerocallis *hybrids*
- Hostas
- Iris laevigata
- Iris pseudacorus
- Iris sibirica
- Cardiocrinum giganteum
- Ligularia dentata (Senecio clivorum)
- Lysichiton americanus
- Lysichiton camtschatcensis
- Lysimachia punctata
- Peltiphyllum peltatum
- Rodgersia pinnata
- Scrophularia aquatica
- Trollius *x* hybridus

CALTHA PALUSTRIS
(Marsh Marigold/ Kingcup)
grows 30–38cm/ 12–15in
high and creates a mass of
cup-shaped, bright yellow
flowers during late spring
and early summer. Space
plants 23–30cm/ 9–12in
apart. As well as being
grown in moist soil at
a pond's edge, it can be
planted in water up to
10cm/ 4in deep.

ARUNCUS DIOICUS
(Goat's Beard) grows
1.2–1.8m/ 4–6ft high
and reveals large, lax
plumes of creamy white
flowers during early and
mid-summer. Position
plants 45–60cm/
1½–2ft apart. It is
especially attractive when
planted near a pond.
Moist, partial shade
suits it best. It is often
also called A. sylvester.

RHEUM ALEXANDRAE
(Ornamental Rhubarb)
grows 75–90cm/ 2½–
3ft high and during early
summer produces erect
flower spikes, up to
45cm/ 18in long, packed
with paper-like, creamy
bracts. In many ways they
resemble drooping tongues.
Space plants 50–60cm/
20–24in apart. It grows
best in fertile, continuously
moist soil.

EUPATORIUM PURPUREUM *(Joe-pye Weed/Hemp Agrimony)* grows 1.2–1.8m/4–6ft high and develops slender, dark stems and terminal clusters, about 10cm/4in wide, of rose-purple flowers during mid and late summer. The variety 'Atropurpureum' has purple leaves and rosy-lilac flowers. Space plants 75–90cm/2¹¹/²–3ft apart. Plant in sun or partial shade.

GIANT LEAVES

Few herbaceous plants are as eye-catching as Gunnera manicata, *with its large, rhubarb-like leaves up to 3m/10ft across. It is ideal for planting right at the edge of a lake or a very large pond. Although* G. manicata *is the species most commonly grown, others are available. Gunneras, by the way, were named by the famous Swedish botanist Linnaeus in honour of Ernest Gunnera, a bishop in Norway who published a Norwegian flora.*

LIGULARIA *'Gregynog Gold' (Golden Groundsel)* grows 90cm–1.2m/3–4ft high, with large leaves around its base and orange-gold flowers from late summer into early autumn. Space plants 45cm/18in apart.

FILIPENDULA PURPUREA *(Dropwort, and also known as* Filipendula palmata *and* Spiraea palmata*)* grows 60cm–1.2m/2–4ft high with tiny, carmine-rose flowers during mid-summer. Space plants 38–45cm/15–18in apart.

RANUNCULUS ACONIFIFOLIUS *'Flore-pleno' (Fair Maids of France)* grows about 60cm/2ft high and has shining, pure white, button-like flowers during early summer. Ensure that the soil does not dry out. Space the plants 30–38cm/12–15in apart.

THALICTRUM SPECIOSISSIMUM *(Dusty Meadow Rue)* grows 90cm–1.5m/3–5ft high and develops huge heads of fluffy yellow flowers during mid and late summer. The leaves are also attractive, deeply divided and blue-grey. Space plants 50–60cm/20–24in apart. Fertile, moisture-retentive soil is essential.

CHALKY SOILS

❖

HALKY soils are difficult to make less alkaline, especially if the underlying layers are rich in chalk. Raised beds, perhaps 30cm/12in above the general level, can be created, but on an entire garden scale this is not practical and could be prohibitively expensive. Digging in well-decayed compost, peat or manure reduces alkalinity, but the effect is soon lost if the soil water is extremely chalky. The long-term solution is to select plants that survive in chalky conditions. Some of the many excellent plants to choose from are suggested here.

Many gardeners spray chemicals on certain trees or shrubs to compensate for the soil type, but this is not really practical with herbaceous plants.

OTHER PLANTS

- Acanthus mollis
- Achillea ptarmica
- Anchusa azurea
- Asphodeline lutea
- Crambe cordifolia
- Echinops ritro
- Eremurus robusta
- Erigeron speciosum
- Gypsophila paniculata
- Helenium autumnale
- Hemerocallis *hybrids*
- Kniphofia – *range of species and varieties*
- Limonium latifolium
- Lychnis chalcedonica
- Rudbeckia hirta
- Verbascum *x* hybridum
- Veronica spicata

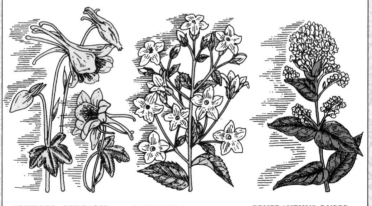

AQUILEGIA VULGARIS *(Columbine/ Granny's Bonnet) grows about 45cm/ 18in high and develops blue, pink, yellow, crimson or white flowers during early summer. Space plants 25– 30cm/ 10–12in apart. The McKana hybrids are especially popular and widely grown, with beautiful long spurs on their flowers.*

CAMPANULA LACTIFLORA *grows 90cm–1.5m/ 3–5ft high and develops light lavender blue, bell-shaped flowers during early and mid-summer. Space the plants 38cm/ 15in apart. There are several superb varieties, including 'Loddon Anna' (flesh pink) and 'Pritchard's Variety' (deep blue).*

CENTRANTHUS RUBER *(Red Valerian) grows 45–90cm/ 1 1/2–3ft high and develops red or deep pink, star-shaped flowers from early to late summer. Space plants 30cm/ 12in apart. Varieties include 'Coccineus' (deep red flowers) and 'Albus'(white). In previous years, centranthus was known as kentranthus,*

CORYDALIS LUTEA

(Yellow Fumitory) grows 15–25cm/6–10in high, with masses of yellow flowers from spring to late autumn. Space plants 25–30cm/10–12in apart. It often grows in old walls, where its colour is most welcome. It has the tendency, however, to seed itself and to produce copious seedlings.

GAILLARDIA ARISTATA

(Blanket Flower) grows 60–75cm/2–2¹¹/2ft high and reveals masses of large, daisy-like, yellow and red flowers about 7.5cm/3in wide from early to late summer. Space the plants 38cm/15in apart. Varieties include 'Dazzler'(orange-yellow and maroon-red) and 'Mandarin' (orange and red).

HELLEBORUS

ORIENTALIS *(Lenten Rose) grows about 45cm/18in high and develops saucer-shaped, cream flowers flecked with crimson during late winter and early spring. This plant has a promiscuous nature and has yielded flowers from white to pink. Ideally, plant it close to the edge of a path.*

DORONICUM

PLANTAGINEUM *(Leopard's Bane) grows 45–50cm/18–20in high and develops golden-yellow flowers about 6cm/2¹/2in wide during late spring and early summer. Space plants 30–38cm/12–15in apart. Varieties include 'Miss Mason' (yellow).*

GEUM CHILOENSE

(Avens) grows 45–60cm/1¹/2–2ft high and develops bowl-shaped flowers from early to late summer. Space plants 30–38cm/12–15in apart. Varieties include 'Lady Stratheden' (double, yellow) and 'Mrs. Bradshaw' (semi-double and scarlet). Popular and widely grown.

IRIS GERMANICA

(London Flag/Purple Flag) grows 60–75cm/2–2¹/2ft tall and develops rich blue flowers during early summer. There are short types (25–45cm/10–18in high) and tall ones (45–75cm/1¹/2–2¹/2ft). 'Golden Fair' (above) is short, with beautiful deep yellow flowers.

SANDY SOILS

❖

THESE soils are light, easy to dig and prepare, but invariably lack plant foods and especially bulky organic material such as manure and compost that would help retain both moisture and nutrients. Also, because such soils are well aerated, organic material soon decays.

IMPROVING SANDY SOIL

When preparing a border, dig in well-decayed compost or manure to enable moisture to be retained. Also, in spring, water the soil thoroughly and form a 5–7.5cm/2–3in-thick mulch of well-decayed compost over bare soil between plants. This prevents moisture evaporating from the surface and returns nutrients to the soil. It also helps to keep the soil cool.

OTHER PLANTS

- Achillea filipendulina
- Achillea clypeolata
- Achillea taygetea
- Alstroemeria *'Ligtu-hybrids'*
- Anaphalis triplinervis
- Anthemis tinctoria
- Bergenia cordifolia
- Catananche caerulea
- Centaurea dealbata
- Centranthus ruber
- Crambe cordifolia
- Dictamnus albus
- Echinops ritro
- Eryngium maritimum
- Gypsophila paniculata
- Polygonum affine
- Stachys byzantina
- Verbascum x hybridum

ANCHUSA AZUREA *(Bugloss/Alkanet) grows 90cm–1.5m/3–5ft high. Bright blue, salver-shaped flowers appear during early and mid-summer. Space plants 30–38cm/12–15in apart. Varieties include 'Loddon Royalist' (gentian blue), 'Dropmore' and 'Morning Glory' (both deep blue).*

ANAPHALUS YEDOENSIS *(Pearl Everlasting) grows about 60cm/2ft high, with grey-green leaves and bunched heads of small, white flowers from mid to late summer. Space plants 30–38cm/12–15in apart. It is ideal for planting in dry, sandy soil, and can be used in flower arrangements.*

ANTHEMIS CUPANIANA *grows 60–30cm/8–12in high and develops daisy-like white flowers with yellow centres during early and mid-summer. These are borne above finely dissected, aromatic, grey leaves. Space plants 25cm/10in apart. It creates good displays in containers as well as beds.*

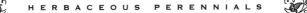

ASPHODELINE LUTEA *(King's Spear) grows about 1.2m/4ft high and develops stiff spikes of fragrant, sulphur yellow flowers during early and mid-summer. Space plants 45cm/1½ft apart. Earlier, this plant was known as* Asphodelus luteus *and is known as Asphodel and, in North America, as Jacob's Rod. It is very distinctive plant and should not be hidden behind other plants.*

LIMONIUM LATIFOLIUM *(Statice/Sea Lavender) has a woody root-stock and grows 45–60cm/1½–2ft high. During mid and late summer it develops lavender blue flowers in heads up to 23cm/9in wide. Space plants 45cm/18in apart. The variety 'Violetta' has violet flowers. Flowers can be easily dried.*

CYNARA CARDUNCULUS *(Cardoon) grows 1.5–2.1m/5–7ft high and develops large, blue or purple flower heads during mid and late summer. Space plants 90cm/3ft apart. Large, prickly leaves, white beneath.*

ERIGERON SPECIOSUS *(Fleabane) grows about 45cm/18in high and develops clusters of daisy-like purple flowers from early to late summer. Space plants 30cm/12in apart. Varieties include 'Darkest of All' (violet-blue), 'Felicity' (pink), 'Foerster's Liebling'(deep pink), 'Gaiety' (bright pink) and 'Quakeress' (mauve-pink).*

BURNING BUSH

Fragrant, white flowers

Variously known as Bastard Dittany, Dittany, Fraxinella and Gas Plant, the Burning Bush (Dictamnus albus) *was introduced into Britain from Europe during the reign of Queen Elizabeth I, in the sixteenth century. The plant owes part of its fame to the flower spikes which have minute reddish-brown glands that secrete an etheric oil which is strongest when the flower is fading. If a lighted match is set against the flower it responds with a reddish, crackling flame.*

CLAY SOILS

❖

CLAY soils are notoriously heavy and difficult to cultivate, as well as being wet and cold. However, they are usually richer in plant foods than sandy soils, where nutrients are rapidly leached out of the topsoil.

Many herbaceous perennials grow in clay soil, but ensure it is well drained so that it is not continually wet during winter, which encourages roots to decay and prevents rapid warming in spring. For this reason, clay soils are frequently described as 'late'.

Before planting herbaceous plants, dig the soil thoroughly and deeply, breaking up the subsoil but ensuring soil from different levels is not mixed. When digging, mix plenty of manure and compost into the soil. This will aid drainage and improve fertility.

OTHER PLANTS

- Achillea filipendulina
- Alchemilla mollis
- Centaurea dealbata
- Centaurea montana
- Coreopsis verticillata
- Epimedium pinnatum
- Epimedium x rubrum
- Hostas – *range of species and varieties*
- Ligularia dentata (Senecio clivorum)
- Macleaya cordata
- Phlomis fruticosa
- Polemonium caeruleum
- Potentilla – *Garden Hybrids*
- Rheum palmatum
- Sidalcea malviflora
- Stachys byzantina (S. olympica/S. lanata)

ASTER x FRIKARTII *grows 60–75cm/ 2–2¹/₂ft high and has dark green leaves and orange-centred, 5cm/ 2in-wide, blue flowers from mid-summer to autumn. It is a hybrid between* A. amellus *and* A. thomsonii. *Most other asters will also survive in clay soil, but ensure it is not at all waterlogged.*

ASTRANTIA MAJOR *(Masterwort) grows 50– 60cm/ 20–24in high and develops star-like, greenish pink flowers during early and mid-summer. Space plants 30–38cm/ 12–15in apart. Other astrantias include* A. carniolica, *with white, star-like flowers tinged pink during mid and late summer.*

CRAMBE CORDIFOLIA *(Colewort) grows 1.5– 1.8m/ 5–6ft high and develops broad, heart-shaped leaves and widely branching stems that bear countless white flowers during early summer. Space plants 90cm–1.2m/ 3–4ft apart. It is ideal for planting at the backs of borders, where it creates a dramatic display.*

PLATYCODON
GRANDIFLORUM *(Balloon
Flower) grows 30–60cm/
1–2ft high, with blue
flowers in summer. Plant
about 38cm/15in apart.*

SIDALCEA MALVIFLORA
*grows 75cm–1.2m/
2½–4ft high, with flowers
throughout summer. Space
45cm/18in apart.*

HEMEROCALLIS
HYBRIDS *(Day Lilies) grow
60–90cm/2–3ft high and
bear a wealth of flowers up
to 18cm/7in wide. Space
plants 45cm/18in apart.
There are many varieties.*

LYSIMACHIA
PUNCTATA *(Yellow
Loosestrife) grows
60–75cm/2–2½ft high
and develops spires of bright
yellow, cup-shaped flowers
from early to late summer.
Space plants 38–45cm/
15–18in apart.*

RUDBECKIA FULGIDA
*(Coneflower) grows 60–
90cm/2–3ft high and
develops large, daisy-like,
yellow to orange flowers
from mid to late summer.
Space plants 45–50cm/
18–20in apart.*

GERANIUM PRATENSE
*'Johnson's Blue' (Meadow
Crane's-bill) grows 38cm/
15in high and develops
light blue flowers from mid-
summer to autumn. Space
plants 38cm/15in apart.
There are several other
superb species and varieties,
some with double flowers.*

ICELANDIC DYE

*The flowers of Meadow Crane's-bill, native to
much of the Northern Hemisphere, are said to
have been used in Iceland to create a blue-grey
dye for the clothing of the heroes of the sagas.
Early names include Odin's Grace and Odin's
Favour, as well as* Gratia Dei, *a translation
of the German word* Gottesgnade.

COASTAL AREAS

❖

ALT-LADEN wind and strong and violent gusts are the problems affecting gardening in coastal areas. Many plants can survive these conditions, but they need a good start in life and this includes creating a screen to protect them from strong winds. Hedges and, on a large scale, screens of pine trees can be used, but these take some time to become established.

On a shorter time scale, temporary wattle-hurdles and canvas screens enable roots of small plants to become established. Other ways to assist plants include improving soil to speed up root establishment, staking plants and mulching in spring. Also, it is beneficial to put plants in small groups, so that each is able to offer protection to its neighbour.

OTHER PLANTS

- Anemone *x* hybrida
- Armeria plantaginea (A. pseudarmeria)
- Catananche caerulea
- Cynara scolymus
- Cynoglossum nervosum
- Crambe cordifolia
- Echinops ritro
- Eryngium giganteum
- Eryngium maritimum
- Eryngium planum
- Euphorbia wulfenii
- Limonium latifolium
- Lychnis coronaria
- Myosotidium hortensia
- Salvia superba
- Scrophularia aquatica
- Sedum spectabile
- Stachys byzantina

ASTER AMELLUS *(Italian Aster) grows 45–60cm/1¹/2–2ft high and creates a mass of 5cm/2in-wide, daisy-like flowers during late summer and into autumn. Space plants 38cm/15in apart. Varieties include 'King George' (violet-blue) and 'Sonia' (rose-pink).*

CENTAUREA MACROCEPHALA *grows 90cm–1.5m/3–5ft high and develops stout stems that produce yellow, thistle-like flowers about 7.5cm/3in wide during early and mid-summer. The leaves are rough and light green. Space plants 50–60cm/20–24in apart. Position it at the back of a border.*

ERYNGIUM ALPINUM *is 45–60cm/1¹/2–2ft high and develops greenish blue leaves around its base. From mid-summer to early autumn it reveals steel blue flowers. Space plants 30–38cm/12–15in apart. The flowers are ideal for winter flower decorations.*

EUPHORBIA GRIFFITHII
*is 60–75cm/2–2¹/2ft high
and develops flame-like bracts
in clusters up to 10cm/4in
across during early summer.
Space plants 50–60cm/
20–24in apart. Varieties
include 'Fireglow' (brilliant
flame orange) and 'Dixter'
(orange-red). After flowering,
the bracts fade to green.*

OLD-AGE ELIXIR

*Eryngiums were grown in Elizabethan gardens,
but the European native Sea Holly* (Eryngium
maritimum) *was used medicinally. In the late
sixteenth century it was said that the roots,
when preserved with sugar,* 'are exceeding
good to be given to old and aged people
that are consumed and withered with
age, and which want natural moisture'.

PHLOMIS RUSSELIANA
*grows 75cm-1.2m/
2¹/2-4ft high and reveals
whorls of yellow flowers
during early and mid-
summer. Space plants about
38cm/15in apart. The
Jerusalem Sage (P. fruti-
cosa) also has similar
whorls of brighter
yellow flowers.*

KNIPHOFIA HYBRIDS
*(Torch Lily/Red Hot Poker)
range in height from 45cm/
1¹/2ft to 1.5m/5ft high.
They all create poker-like
heads, in colours including
yellow, orange and red. Plant
them about two-thirds of
their height apart.*

DIERAMA
PULCHERRIMUM *(Wand
Flower/Angel's Fishing Rod)
grows 1.2–1.5m/4–5ft high
and develops deep red flowers
from mid-summer to autumn.
Space plants about 38cm/
15in apart. Varieties include
shades of pink, purple and
violet, as well as white.*

VERONICA SPICATA
*grows 15–45cm/6–18in
high and develops dense,
terminal spires of blue
flowers from early to the
end of summer. Varieties
include 'Barcarolle' (rose
pink). 'Crater Lake Blue'
(ultramarine blue),
'Pavane' (deep pink) and
'Heidekind' (beautiful,
glowing deep pink).*

49

ATTRACTIVE FOLIAGE

❖

THESE plants have colourful or attractively shaped leaves – or both. Some, such as Lady's Mantle *(Alchemilla mollis)*, have a gentle and demure appearance, while others, like *Ophiopogon plansicapus* 'Nigrescens', are dominantly coloured and if used too frequently in a border can be overpowering to the eye. They also tend to dominate other plants and therefore must be used with great care if they are not to be obtrusive.

Several of these plants agreeably nestle alongside path and border edges; they include Lady's Mantle, Bergenia cordifolia, *Astilbe* x *arendsii* and *Festuca glauca*. Others grow higher and need more space. These include *Scrophularia aquatica* 'Variegata', *Euphorbia characias* and *Rodgersia podophyllum*.

OTHER PLANTS

- Acanthus mollis
- Aegopodium podagraria 'Variegata'
- Anaphalis triplinervis
- Artemisia lactiflora
- Artemisia ludoviciana
- Cynara cardunculus
- Epimedium perralderianum
- Epimedium x rubrum
- Hosta – *wide range*
- Melissa officinalis *'Aurea'*
- Pulmonaria saccharata *'Leopard'*
- Pulmonaria saccharata *'Argentea'*
- Stachys byzantina
- Tiarella cordifolia

ALCHEMILLA MOLLIS *(Lady's Mantle) grows 30–45cm/ 12–18in high, with light green, hairy leaves surmounted from early to mid-summer by yellowish green, star-shaped flowers. Space these spectacular plants 30–38cm/12–15in apart. Ideal for edging paths.*

BERGENIA CORDIFOLIA *grows 30cm/ 12in high, with mid-green, glossy, rounded leaves with a heart-shaped base. During mid and late spring it develops clusters of bell-shaped, lilac-rose flowers. Space plants 30–38cm/ 12–15in apart.*

ASTILBE x ARENDSII *grows 60–75cm/ 2–2½ft high, with fern-like, deep green leaves and lax, pyramidal spires of flowers during early and mid-summer. Space plants 38cm/ 15in apart. There are many colours including red, pink and white.*

OPHIOPOGON
PLANSICAPUS *'Nigrescens'*
grows about 20cm/8in high
and develops narrow black
leaves. White-tinged violet
flowers appear during
summer, followed by purple-
black berries. Space plants
30cm/12in apart. Plant in
well-drained, fertile soil.

EUPHORBIA
CHARACIAS *grows*
90cm–1m/3–4ft high,
with blue-grey, oblong
leaves. During early
summer the leaves are
surmounted by sulphur
yellow flowers and paper-
like bracts. Space plants
75–90cm/2½–3ft apart.

SCROPHULARIA
AQUATICA *'Variegata'*
(Water Figwort), grows
90cm/3ft and displays
green leaves attractively
splashed and striped
cream. Space these hand-
some plants 38–45cm/
15–18in apart.

RODGERSIA
PODOPHYLLA
grows 90cm–1.2m/
3–4ft high and
displays mid-green,
horse-chestnut-like
leaves and pale buff
flowers during early
and mid-summer. Space
plants 60cm/2ft apart.
R. pinnata *has deep
green leaves.*

FESTUCA GLAUCA *is
an ornamental grass, about
23cm/9in high and with
blue-grey leaves. During
early and mid-summer,
purple spikelets appear on
stems about 30cm/12in
long. Space plants 15–
23cm/6–9in apart. It is
superb when three or five
plants are grown in a
cluster near to a path's
edge, especially at the
junction of two paths.*

HANDSOME RUE

*For centuries, Rue (Ruta graveolens) was
used as an antiseptic and antidote to poisons.
During the seventeenth and eighteenth centuries it
was strewn in law courts as protection against
gaol fever. However, it also has very attractive
leaves; the variety 'Jackson's Blue' forms a neat
mound about 45cm/18in high of bright, blue-
grey leaves. Although strictly an evergreen shrub,
it is frequently grown in herbaceous borders.*

CUT FLOWERS FOR HOME DECORATION

❖

Herbaceous plants are ideal for providing flowers to fill vases indoors in summer. Most flowers are cut from plants growing in borders, but to prevent them being spoiled – and if space allows – grow a few in an out-of-the-way corner.

Never cut flowers for home decoration from wilting plants. In fact, the ideal way is to water the plants thoroughly and to cut the flowers early the following morning, before the full force of the sun reaches them. Cut the stems at a 45-degree angle and remove the lower leaves. Then, place the stems in a bucket of deep, cool water for twenty-four hours before arranging them. Special additives can be put in the water to encourage the flowers to last longer.

OTHER PLANTS

- Achillea ptarmica
- Acontinum napellus
- Aster amellus
- Aster novi-belgii
- Centaurea dealbata
- Doronicum plantagineum
- Echinops ritro
- Gaillardia aristata
- Gypsophila paniculata
- Liatris spicata
- Limonium latifolium
- Lychnis chalcedonica
- Phlox paniculata
- Physostegia virginiana
- Pyrethrum – *hybrid varieties*
- Rudbeckia laciniata
- Scabiosa caucasica
- Solidago – *Garden Hybrids*

ACHILLEA FILIPENDULINA *(Fern-leaf Yarrow)* grows 90cm–1.2m/3–4ft high and develops 10–15cm/4–6in-wide heads of lemon yellow flowers from mid to late summer. Space plants 75–90cm/2½–3ft apart. 'Coronation Gold' has deep yellow flowers from early to late summer.

AGAPANTHUS 'Headbourne Hybrids' *(African Lily)* grow 60–75cm/2–2½ft high and develop violet-blue to pale blue flowers in umbrella-like heads from mid to late summer. These hybrids are slightly hardier than the species types. Space these distinctive plants 38–45cm/15–18in apart.

ALSTROEMERIA 'Ligtu Hybrids' *(Peruvian Lily)* grow 60–75cm/2–2½ft high and develop masses of trumpet-shaped flowers in pink, scarlet, flame, orange, yellow and white from early to late summer. Space plants 30cm/12in apart. They are ideal for room decoration, as well as creating bright displays in borders.

CATANANCHE
CAERULEA *(Cupid's Dart)
grows 45–60cm/1¹/2–2ft
high and has blue flowers
during early and mid-
summer. Varieties include
'Major' (deep lavender blue)
and 'Alba' (white). Space
plants 30–38cm/12–15in
apart. The flowers can be
displayed fresh or dried.*

CHRYSANTHEMUM
MAXIMUM *(Shasta Daisy)
grows 75–90cm/2¹/2–3ft
high and develops white
flowers up to 7.5cm/3in
wide from early to late
summer. Space plants 38cm/
15in apart. Varieties include
'Horace Read' (creamy
white), 'Wirral Pride' (semi-
double/white).*

COREOPSIS
VERTICILLATA *grows
45–60cm/1¹/2–2ft high,
with finely divided, somewhat
fern-like, bright green leaves.
Throughout summer it bears
yellow flowers. Space plants
30–38cm/12–15in apart.
Varieties include
'Grandiflora' (rich yellow)
and 'Zagreb' (golden yellow).*

LUPINS *'Russell Strain'
grow about 90cm/3ft high
and create long spires of pea-
like flowers during early and
mid-summer. Space plants
60–75cm/2–2¹/2ft apart.
The wide range of varieties
includes white, blue, red, pink
and yellow.*

LYSIMACHIA PUNCTATA
*(Yellow Loosestrife) grows
60–75/2–2¹/2ft high and
develops bright yellow flowers
in large clusters, up to
38cm/15in long from early
to late summer. Space plants
38–45cm/15–18in apart.*

ZANTEDESCHIA
AETHIOPICA
*'Crowborough' (Arum Lily)
grows 45–75cm/1¹/2–
2¹/2ft high and produces
white flowers during mid to
late summer. Space plants
38–45cm/15–18in apart.*

FLOWERS AND
SEED-HEADS FOR DRYING

❖

IN ADDITION to evergreen shrubs and climbers, such as holly and ivy that brighten Christmas and the New Year, dried flowers and seed-heads of herbaceous perennials can also make very attractive features. And once dried they usually last throughout winter.

Cut the stems either just as the flowers are fully formed or, for seed-heads, when they start to change colour. Cut off the stems and hang them upside-down in a well-ventilated, slightly warm, dry room. Leave them until all moisture has gone, but avoid drying them too quickly. Then, remove and discard the parts not needed and arrange the selected pieces in vases or special displays. Do not allow dust to spoil them.

STINKING IRIS

The Stinking Iris (Iris foetidissima), *also now known as Stinking Gladdon and Gladwyn, was referred to in the sixteenth century as Xyris and Spourgwurt, because of its purgative qualities. Powdered, dried roots have been used to relieve pains and cramps, and also for hysterical disorders, fainting and nervous complaints. A more appealing name than Stinking Iris is Roast Beef, on account of its leaves which, when bruised, smell agreeably like hot, roast meat. The flowers are followed by seed pods which, when ripe, have orange-red seeds.*

ACANTHUS MOLLIS
(Bear's Breeches) grows 90cm/3ft high, with large, wavy-edged leaves and 30cm/12in-long spikes of white and purple flowers during mid and late summer. Space plants 50–60cm/ 20–24in apart. The flower-heads can be dried for display during winter.

PHYSALIS ALKEKENGI
(Chinese Lantern/Bladder Cherry) grows 30–38cm/ 12–15in high and develops white flowers followed by 5cm/2in-long, bright red lantern-like cases. Cut the stems when the lanterns show colour and hang in an airy, dry room. Space plants 45cm/18in apart.

DICTAMNUS ALBUS
(Burning Bush) grows 60cm/2ft high and develops spikes of white, spider-like flowers during early and mid-summer. Space plants 38–45cm/15–18in apart. When the pods are formed, cut the stems and hang them upside down in a dry, dust-free, airy room.

ECHINOPS RITRO *(Globe Thistle) grows 90cm–1.2m/ 3–4ft high, with steel blue flowers during mid and late summer. Space plants 45cm/18in apart.*

GYPSOPHILA PANICULATA *(Baby's Breath) grows 60–90cm/ 2–3ft high and develops lax heads of white flowers throughout summer. Space plants 75cm/2¹/2ft apart.*

PAPAVER ORIENTALE *(Oriental Poppy) grows 60–90cm/2–3ft high and during early summer develops scarlet flowers. These are followed by seed-heads that can be dried. Space plants 50–60cm/20–24in apart.*

ONOPORDUM ACANTHIUM *(Scotch Thistle) grows 1.2– 1.8m/4–6ft high and has pale purple flowers. Space plants 60–75cm/ 2–2¹/2ft apart. Although a perennial, it is sometimes grown as a biennial in cold regions.*

STACHYS BYZANTINA *(Lamb's Tongue) grows 30–45cm/12–18in high and develops purple flowers during mid-summer. These can be dried. Space plants 30–45cm/12–18in apart.*

IRIS FOETIDISSIMA *(Stinking Iris/Gladwyn Iris) grows 50cm/20in high and develops insignificant purple flowers during early summer. Later, seed pods appear. Space plants 30–45cm/ 1–1¹/2ft apart. Cut the stems and hang them upside-down to dry, then use for winter decoration indoors.*

OTHER PLANTS

- Acanthus spinosus *(Bear's Breeches)*
- Anaphalis triplinervis *(Pearl Everlasting)*
- Cynara cardunculus *(Cardoon)*
- Delphinium elatum
- Eryngium – *several species*
- Iris ochroleuca *(Butterfly Iris)*
- Limonium latifolium *(Sea Lavender)*

FOR GROWING IN TUBS

❖

PATIOS and paved areas in gardens play an important role, forming all-weather surfaces and enabling plants in tubs and pots to be grown immediately around a house. Shrubs, small trees, miniature conifers and many bulbs are the best candidates for these positions, but so are some herbaceous perennials.

The difficulties of growing herbaceous plants in tubs and pots is that the compost is likely to become too warm in summer and much too wet and cold in winter. Some plants, such as hostas, prefer light shade and this helps to prevent compost becoming excessively warm. Also, wooden tubs keep compost cool in summer and warm in winter.

OTHER PLANTS

- Alchemilla mollis
- Crocosmia x crocosmiiflora
- Epimedium *'Frohnleiten'*
- Heuchera *'Pewter Moon'*
- Houttuynia cordata *'Chameleon'*
- Liatris spicata *'Kobold'*
- Lilium formosanum
- Melissa officinalis *'All Gold'*
- Polygonum affine *'Dimity'*
- Salvia officinalis *'Icterina'*
- Salvia officinalis *'Purpurescens'*
- Stachys byzantina *'Primrose Heron'*

AEGOPODIUM PODOGARIA *'Variegata'* is a variegated form of the infamous Ground Elder. It grows 15–23cm/6–9in high and reveals green leaves with white edges. Because it is so invasive, ensure that it stays in a tub or large pot.

AGAPANTHUS *'Lilliput'* is a relatively diminutive African Lily, bearing dainty, bright blue, trumpet-like flowers about 15cm/6in across during mid-summer. For a bolder display, plant A. campanulatus *'Isis'* .

ARUNDINARIA VIRIDISTRIATA is a 75cm–1.2m/2½–4ft-high bamboo, ideal for growing in pots and tubs. Upright stems bear rich variegated leaves that retain their attractiveness throughout the year.

HAKONECHLOA MACRA *'Albo-aurea'* is an attractively cascading grass with graceful, ribbon-like leaves vividly variegated buff and gold, with touches of bronze. Plant it in a tub or large pot and position where its shape is uncluttered by other plants. Place in full sun or light shade.

DICENTRA *'Snowflakes'*, a Bleeding Heart, grows about 25cm/10in high and is therefore ideal for growing in small pots on a patio, where it readily attracts bees and develops clusters of pendulous white flowers throughout summer. The finely divided, light green leaves create a superb backdrop for the flowers. Position it in full sun or light shade.

BERGENIA *'Bressingham Ruby'* is a patio plant for all seasons. In winter its large, elephant-ear-like, green leaves turn burnished maroon, while its deep rosy red flowers brighten spring. It grows 30–38cm/12–15in high and can be positioned in full sun or light shade. Avoid damaging the leaves.

HOSTA *'Wide Brim'* has green leaves beautifully edged in cream to golden yellow. Take care that its leaves are not knocked, as they may then become torn. Another hosta for containers is *'Shade Fanfare'*, with green leaves edged in cream. The green often lightens when the plant is in full sun.

PERILOUS JOURNEYS

Botanists who searched for new plants often had to endure extreme hardships, ranging from hostile natives to inhospitable terrain. The Scottish plant collector, David Douglas, searched in North America during the 1800s and discovered many plants now popular in gardens. On his way home in 1834 he went to Hawaii, fell into a pit-trap and was fatally maimed by a bull already in residence.

The dying David Douglas with his friends and faithful dog.

PESTS AND DISEASES

❖

Each spring and early summer, herbaceous plants create a diet of soft stems, leaves and buds for insects to suck and chew. They are also a temptation to diseases. Garden hygiene is essential:

• In winter, prepare the ground for new flower beds by digging deeply to expose soil pests for birds or frost to kill.

• Remove weeds, as they harbour pests and diseases throughout summer, also enabling them to survive the winter.

• Throughout summer, shallowly hoe between plants.

• Spray or dust with insecticides to control pests as soon as they are seen. Do not wait until they become a major problem.

• In autumn, remove old stems and leaves to ensure they will not enable pests and diseases to survive the winter.

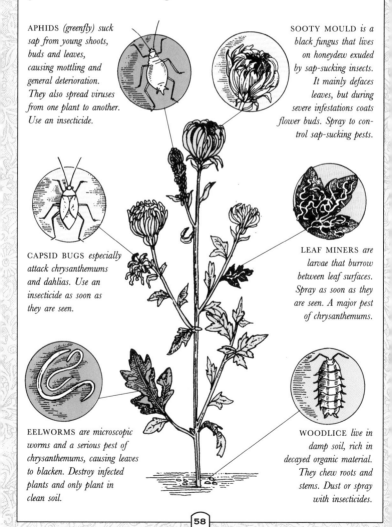

APHIDS *(greenfly) suck sap from young shoots, buds and leaves, causing mottling and general deterioration. They also spread viruses from one plant to another. Use an insecticide.*

SOOTY MOULD *is a black fungus that lives on honeydew exuded by sap-sucking insects. It mainly defaces leaves, but during severe infestations coats flower buds. Spray to control sap-sucking pests.*

CAPSID BUGS *especially attack chrysanthemums and dahlias. Use an insecticide as soon as they are seen.*

LEAF MINERS *are larvae that burrow between leaf surfaces. Spray as soon as they are seen. A major pest of chrysanthemums.*

EELWORMS *are microscopic worms and a serious pest of chrysanthemums, causing leaves to blacken. Destroy infected plants and only plant in clean soil.*

WOODLICE *live in damp soil, rich in decayed organic material. They chew roots and stems. Dust or spray with insecticides.*

CATERPILLARS *chew tender leaves, stems and flower buds. Pick them off and spray regularly with a suitable insecticide.*

POWDERY MILDEW *is a fungus that coats leaves of chrysanthemums, Michaelmas Daisies, delphiniums and limoniums with a white mould. Use fungicides.*

LEAFY GALL *is caused by a bacterial disease: gall-like growths cluster on stems and leaves. Destroy seriously infected plants.*

EARWIGS *chew and shred petals and leaves, especially those of dahlias and chrysanthemums. Trap in pots filled with straw and inverted on canes. Also, spray with insecticides.*

CUTWORMS *live in the topsoil and chew stems, causing plants to collapse and die. Dust the soil with an insecticide. Also, pick up and destroy them.*

FROG HOPPERS *infest many herbaceous plants, creating froth-like foam on stems and around flower buds. This surrounds young frog hoppers that suck sap. Use an insecticide.*

MILLEPEDES *have two pairs of legs on each body segment; they move slowly and eat roots and stems. Dust with insecticides.*

WIREWORMS *are the larvae of click beetles. They are long, cylindrical and have three pairs of legs. Dust with an insecticide and regularly hoe topsoil.*

SLUGS AND SNAILS *are especially damaging during warm, wet summer nights, when they emerge and chew plants. Use baits to kill them (position away from cats and dogs).*

HERBACEOUS
BORDER CALENDAR
❖

SPRING

This is when herbaceous plants start to grow after being dormant during winter. Take care that young shoots are not damaged by birds, insects, or by a shoe when walking between them.

- In late spring or early summer, sow seeds outdoors in shallow drills in specially prepared seed-beds (14–15).
- Protect newly sown seeds from birds by covering the surface with twiggy sticks or stretching cotton across the bed (14–15).
- Keep the seed-bed moist but not waterlogged (14–15). If the surface dries, the seedlings die.
- Divide herbaceous perennials in spring or autumn. Some plants prefer spring, others autumn, while a few can be increased at either of these times (16–17).
- Do not divide herbaceous perennials into very small pieces, as they then need to be planted into a nurserybed for several years (16–17).
- Take cuttings of delphiniums from healthy plants (18–19).
- In early spring or late winter, take root cuttings of phlox. These are laid horizontally on the surface of compost (18–19).
- In late winter or early spring, take cuttings of dahlias (20–21).
- In late winter or early spring, take cuttings of chrysanthemums (20–21).
- In mid-spring, plant herbaceous perennials (22–23).
- In spring, lightly fork between plants in established herbaceous borders (24–25).
- In late spring, sprinkle fertilizers around plants (24–25).
- In late spring or early summer, form a mulch (24–25).

SUMMER

This is when herbaceous plants flood borders with colour. It is also the time when pests and diseases infest plants, so be sure to inspect them regularly.

- In early summer, as well as late spring, seeds can be sown outdoors in shallow drills in sheltered, specially prepared seed-beds (14–15).
- Protect newly sown seeds from birds by covering the surface with twiggy sticks or stretching cotton across the bed (14–15).
- When seedlings are large enough to handle, thin them (usually in two stages) to ensure those remaining have equal light and space, to develop into strong, healthy plants (14–15).
- Keep the seed-bed moist but not waterlogged (14–15). If the surface dries, the seedlings die.
- Divide the London Flag iris *(Iris germanica)* in summer, after it finishes flowering. Alternatively, divide it in autumn (16–17).
- After dividing plants, keep the soil moist to aid rapid establishment (16–17).
- In early and mid-summer, layer border carnations (16–17).
- In early summer or even late spring (as soon as all risk of frost has passed) divide dahlia tubers which have been stored in a frost-proof shed during winter (20–21). Alternatively, put in new dahlia plants raised from cuttings (20–21).
- In late spring or early summer, form a thick mulch around plants (24–25).
- During early and mid-summer, feed plants (24–25).
- Remove dead flower heads throughout summer (24–25).

AUTUMN

As cold weather becomes more apparent, this is the time for clearing up herbaceous borders. Occasionally, this task is left until early spring, so that patterns created by frost on old stems and leaves can be enjoyed. Also, leaving the stems in place affords some protection for plants that are not fully hardy. Some plants grown in herbaceous borders retain their leaves during winter and create further surfaces for frost patterns. Ensure these plants can be easily seen.

- Divide herbaceous perennials in autumn or spring. Some plants have a preference for autumn, others for spring, while a few can be increased at either of these times (16–17).
- Do not divide herbaceous perennials into very small pieces, as they then need to be planted into a nurserybed for several years (16–17).
- Divide the London Flag iris *(Iris germanica)* in autumn or after it finishes flowering. Alternatively, divide them in summer (16–17).
- After dividing plants, keep the soil moist to aid rapid establishment (16–17).
- Take root-cuttings of plants such as anchusa, lupins and Oriental Poppies during their dormant period, in late autumn and winter (18–19).
- In autumn, cut down and box-up the old roots of chrysanthemums (20–21).
- In autumn, cut down dahlia plants. Place the tubers in a frost-free area where they can be stored during winter (20–21).
- In early to mid-autumn, plant herbaceous perennials (22–23).
- In autumn, cut down herbaceous plants (24–25). Alternatively, leave this job until late winter, after frost displays.

WINTER

All that is apparent in most herbaceous borders at this season is bare soil. Occasionally, however, plants are not cut down until late winter and these are attractive when covered in frost.

- Prepare borders in early winter by single digging them. Double digging is usually only necessary when converting pasture land into a flower garden (12–13).
- Remove and burn perennial weeds while digging (12–13).
- Pick up and destroy soil pests (see pages 12 and 13, as well as 58 and 59 for identification).
- Consider using an automatic digger (12–13).
- When digging wide flower beds, first divide the border into two parts (12–13).
- Take root-cuttings of plants such as anchusa, lupins and Oriental Poppies during their dormant period, in late autumn and winter (18–19).
- In late winter or early spring, take root-cuttings of phlox. These are laid horizontally on the surface of compost (18–19).
- In late winter, re-pack dahlia tubers in boxes of compost and place in gentle warmth (20–21).
- In late winter or early spring, take cuttings of dahlias (20–21).
- In late winter, place chrysanthemum stools (earlier boxed up) in gentle warmth to encourage the development of young shoots to form cuttings (20–21).
- In late winter or early spring, take cuttings of chrysanthemums (20–21).
- In mild areas, planting is still possible (22–23).
- During winter, plan herbaceous borders (22–23). Select a range of plants and send an order to a specialist nursery. Alternatively, buy from garden centres or local nurseries.

GLOSSARY OF
HERBACEOUS BORDER TERMS

❖

BOG GARDEN: *An area, natural or constructed, formed of moist soil. Many herbaceous perennials are suited to these places.*

BRACT: *A modified leaf, sometimes green but often coloured or white, at the base of, or integrated with, a flower. Sometimes, more attractive than the flowers.*

CLONE: *Plants produced vegetatively from a single parent. This ensures that the progeny are identical.*

COMPOST: *This has two meanings. The first is decomposed vegetable material that is either spread on the surface to form a mulch or dug in during winter. The other meaning is a mixture of loam, sand and peat in which seeds can be sown, plants planted or seedlings pricked out.*

CULTIVAR: *A variation in a species or hybrid which has arisen in cultivation. Such a plant is indicated by placing single quotation marks around its name, eg 'Variegata'.*

CUTTING: *A method of propagation, whereby part of a healthy parent plant is removed and encouraged to form roots. Cuttings can be formed from stems, leaves or roots. Because this is a vegetative form of propagation, new plants totally resemble the parent.*

DEAD-HEADING: *The removal of dead or faded flowers to encourage the development of further blooms, thereby extending the flowering period.*

DIVISION: *A method of propagating fibrous-rooted herbaceous perennials by digging up and separating their roots into pieces that can be immediately replanted into borders. Alternatively, if the new pieces are very small they can be put into a nurserybed for a year or so before being planted into a garden border.*

DOUBLE DIGGING: *This is when soil is dug to the depth of two spade blades. However, soil from the upper level must not be mixed with the lower.*

DOUBLE-SIDED BORDERS: *Formed of two equally sized flower beds either side of a wide grass or paved path. Usually, these borders are backed by an evergreen hedge.*

DRILL: *A shallow depression, formed with a draw hoe or pointed stick, in which seeds are sown. In the open ground these drills are usually 6–12mm/ 1/4–1/2 deep and 23cm/ 9in apart.*

F1 HYBRID: *A hybrid plant, raised from crossing two distinct and unrelated parents. Such plants have additional vigour.*

FLORE-PLENA: *Used to describe flowers with a larger than normal number of petals. They are described as semi-double or double.*

FLOWER: *The reproductive part of a plant. It is often highly coloured to attract pollinating insects; alternatively, it may have a sweet scent. Some have a foetid aroma to lure flies.*

FRIABLE: *Soil which is crumbly and can be raked to form a tilth.*

GROUND COVER: *Plants that cover the ground with leaves, preventing the growth of weeds and forming an attractive feature.*

HERBACEOUS PERENNIAL: *A plant that each autumn dies down to ground level and in the following spring develops fresh shoots, leaves and flowers. Some plants from warm countries are not naturally herbaceous, but in temperate regions adopt this method of growth in order to survive the winter.*

HYBRID: *A plant whose parents come from two distinct and different species. When the cross is between two species, this is indicated by placing an x between the generic (first) and specific (second) name. Rarer is a cross between two genera; shown by positioning an X before the generic (first) name.*

ISLAND BEDS: *Usually kidney-shaped, 1.8–2.4m/ 6–8ft wide, and set within a lawn. Sometimes, three of them are used to create a larger feature.*

LAYERING: *A method of propagating woody and soft-stemmed plants. Border carnations are often increased in this way.*

LOAM: *Friable top soil, neither excessively sandy nor clayey, which is used to form compost in which seeds can be sown or seedlings and plants grown.*

MIXED BORDER: *Formed of a range of plants, such as herbaceous perennials, annuals, biennials, bulbs, shrubs and small trees.*

MULCHING: *Forming a layer of well-decayed organic material, such as compost, on the soil's surface to prevent the growth of weeds and to conserve moisture in the soil. In vegetable gardens, black plastic is also used.*

NEUTRAL: *Soil which is neither acid nor alkaline. It has a ph value of 7.0. Most plants grow well in slightly acid soil, with a ph of 6.5.*

PERENNIAL: *Any plant that lives for two or more years. Clearly, this definition applies to trees and shrubs as well as herbaceous plants, but because trees and shrubs are assumed to live for many years the term is most often taken to refer to herbaceous perennials.*

PH: *A method of measuring the acidity or alkalinity of soil. It is indicated on a pH scale from 0 to 14. A reading of pH 7.0 is neutral; figures below this indicate increasing acidity, while above it is alkaline.*

PROPAGATION: *Increasing numbers of plants: usually, this is from seeds, cuttings, division or layering.*

RHIZOME: *An horizontal, underground stem: some are slender, while others are thick and concertina-like. The London Flag iris* (Iris germanica) *has typical thick rhizomes.*

ROOT-CUTTINGS: *A method of increasing plants by cutting up their roots. Thick roots are inserted vertically into compost, thin ones laid horizontally.*

SEED-BED: *A piece of soil, evenly dug and firmed so that seeds can be sown in it. This is done in shallow drills, about 23cm/ 9in apart. The ensuing seedlings are thinned so that the remaining ones have plenty of light, air and space in which to grow. Unthinned seedlings can become etiolated.*

SINGLE DIGGING: *Turning over soil to the depth of a spade's blade, about 25cm/ 10in deep. This is performed in winter, in preparation for planting or sowing seeds (see seed-bed). All perennial weeds must be removed and burned; if left, they grow again during the following year.*

SINGLE-SIDED BORDER: *Traditionally, a border 1.8m/ 6ft or more wide and usually backed by an evergreen hedge.*

SPIT: *The depth of a spade's blade.*

STAKING: *Some herbaceous plants need to be staked, others are self-supporting. Use canes, twiggy sticks or proprietary supports. Ensure that they are functional but unobtrusive, and that when plants are fully clothed with leaves they will be hidden.*

STOOL: *The roots of chrysanthemum plants after they have been cut to about 15cm/ 6in high in autumn. They are put into boxes, with compost around them, and in spring develop shoots which can be used to create new cuttings.*

THINNING: *The process of removing surplus seedlings, so that the remaining ones have more space in which to develop into healthy plants. Sometimes, this is performed in two stages; the first thinning is to half the desired spacing, and later to the full distance. Ensure soil is re-firmed around those seedlings that remain once the surplus seedlings have been removed.*

TILTH: *Fine, crumbly surface soil; this is essential when sowing seeds.*

TUBER: *A swollen, underground food storage organ: some are stem-tubers (such as potatoes), others root-tubers (dahlias).*

INDEX